THE FIRST FAMILY
— OF —
TEXAS
SMOKED MEATS
— BEAR BOTTOM TEXAS —
EST 1943

*But small is the gate and narrow the road
that leads to life, and only a few find it.*

Matthew 7:14

Walker's Mill Road

Bear Bottom Bliss

Five Generations Of Food, Family & Faith

A COUNTRY COOKBOOK FROM
'THE FIRST FAMILY OF TEXAS SMOKED MEATS'™

BY THE SHOULTS FAMILY

CONTENT EDITING, DESIGN, PHOTO & ART DIRECTION
BY CHUCK STOVALL

PHOTOGRAPHY* BY
JIM BOWIE - FOOD & JARED NAVARRE - LOCATION

*RANDOM OTHER PHOTOGRAPHY BY VARIOUS SOURCES

FOUR COLOUR PRINT GROUP

LOUISVILLE, KENTUCKY 40206

PRINTED IN CHINA

LIBRARY OF CONGRESS CIP HAS BEEN APPLIED FOR

ISBN 978-0-692-73780-4

- DEDICATION -

This Country Cookbook Is Dedicated To Our Founders,

'HICK' & NELLIE SHOULTS

*It Has Long Been A Dream Of Ours To Create A Cookbook Celebrating
Our Love Of Food Combined With The Rich History Of Our Family Heritage
Over The Past 70 Plus Years.*

*We Feel This Labor Of Love Reflects All The Joy That Is So Much A Part Of
The Five Generations Of The Shoults Family Here In
Bear Bottom, Texas!*

*We Hope You Will Enjoy These Tall Tales, Reminiscences, And Recipes As Much
As We Have Enjoyed Bringing Them To You!*

Bobby, Robbie & Hunter Shoults

CONTENTS

"This is the one that 'Brung Us To The Dance' as we say in Texas!"

Robbie Shoults

- FORWARD -

The sound of Texas country music coming from the old radio in the living room of the Shoults' house in the fall of 1938 was interrupted by an occasional news flash. The words were usually dire, describing the deteriorating events taking place in Europe, as well as the sobering effects of a country still in the grip of The Great Depression. The once soothing words of FDR assuring everyone that 'the only thing to fear, was fear itself' had faded into the harsh reality of the day-to-day struggle to survive, and was little comfort for those East Texas farmers.

One of those farm families was named Shoults. Hick Shoults had been casting about for most of the 1930's in search of a more profitable crop than cotton or corn. Those markets, as well as the cattle market, had faded in the grip of The Depression.

Jim Shoults, Hick's uncle, was an Agriculture teacher in the Grapeland, Texas area. He had been urging Hick to consider raising turkeys, explaining that it would be more profitable to fatten up turkeys for market than the cattle and hogs Hick had been raising. Hick was convinced. That was 1943.

In their first year, the family raised 640 turkeys on their farm in Bear Bottom, where a small stream called Bear Creek fed into Little Cypress Creek. Each year they increased the number of turkeys produced. The family built their first little processing plant, 'Shoults' Famous Turkeys', shortly after. It was not long before they decided to abandon raising cotton and went into the Smokehouse business full-time!

From that humble beginning, Bear Creek Smokehouse has continued to expand their operation with quality smoked selections and outstanding friendly service... all under the watchful guidance of five generations of the Shoults Family!

This stand of Pines, in Bear Bottom, always brings
back a lot of boyhood memories for me!

Robbie Shoults

- THE SHOULTS FAMILY -

'THE FIRST FAMILY OF TEXAS SMOKED MEATS'

CRANBERRY-GLAZED APPETIZER MEATBALLS

Makes 3 Dozen

1½ pounds lean ground beef

½ cup finely chopped onion

½ cup dried bread crumbs

½ teaspoon salt

⅛ teaspoon black pepper

2 eggs, slightly beaten

3 *(12 ounce)* bottles chili sauce

2 *(16 ounce)* cans jellied cranberry sauce

Fresh cranberries, if desired for garnish

"This appetizer is the perfect touch for almost any get-together. People just love their slightly sweet and tart flavor... always an elegant touch!"
Stacia Shoults

Preheat oven to 375 degrees.

In a large bowl, stir together beef, onion, bread crumbs, salt, pepper, and eggs. Mix well. Shape mixture into 1" diameter balls and place *(not touching)* on 15" x 10" x 1" baking pan. Bake 25-30 minutes or until thoroughly cooked.

While meatballs are baking, make sauce. Place chili sauce and cranberry sauce in three quart saucepan. Bring ingredients to a simmer. Cook about five minutes, stirring often. When meatballs are finished baking, add them to the sauce, stirring to coat meatballs with the sauce. Cook for additional five minutes, stirring occasionally. Serve warm.

Meatballs can be served on toothpicks. To use cranberries as garnish, thread one cranberry on toothpick and stick into meatball. Repeat for all meatballs.

Mississippi Sin

Snacks for 15-20

2 cups *(8 ounces)* shredded cheddar cheese

8 ounces cream cheese, softened

1½ cups sour cream

½ cup diced cooked Bear Creek Smokehouse™ Smoked Ham

1 can chopped green chilies

⅓ cup chopped green onion tops

⅛ teaspoon Worcestershire®

1 round loaf King's Hawaiian® Bread®

"I always have to hand this recipe out when I make it for parties and gatherings! It's so easy-to-make and everyone loves it!"
Tracy Shoults

Preheat oven to 350 degrees.

In a large mixing bowl, combine all ingredients except bread. Mix well. Set aside.

With bread on working surface, cut a thin slice from the top of the loaf. Reserve the slice. Gently hollow out the loaf to leave 1-1½" thick shell and bottom. Save removed bread for future use. ***Return the bread to the tin it came in.*** Fill the hollowed loaf with reserved mixture. Cover with reserved top slice of bread loaf. Cover the bread with aluminum foil, securing to the sides or bottom of the tin. Bake for 1 hour. Serve warm with crackers or chips.

From the kitchen of Minnie Wise

Creamed Pimento Cheese

Appetizers for 4-6

⅔ cup cream cheese, softened

2 Tablespoons minced onion

2 Tablespoons minced bell pepper

1 Tablespoon chopped pimento, drained

1 Tablespoon mayonnaise

2 teaspoons ketchup

1 egg, hard boiled and chopped

In a mixing bowl, combine all ingredients and mix until smooth. The mixture can be served on bread or crackers.

"A scrumptious, little recipe that the kids just love!"
Stacia Shoults

"The beautiful Bluebonnets that appear
every year here in Bear Bottom signal the
return of Spring!"
Stacia Shoults

STACIA'S SKINNY DIPPING

Makes 4-6 servings

1 can of chicken

1 red bell pepper, seeds removed and finely diced

2 jalapeños, seeds removed and minced

1 can whole kernel corn, drained

¼ cup black or green olives, drained and chopped

16 ounces fat-free cream cheese, softened

1 packet Hidden Valley® Ranch dip seasoning mix

In a large bowl, combine all ingredients. Mix until thoroughly combined. Serve room temperature or chilled. Serve with crackers or vegetable sticks.

"This is a fun, refreshing dip that's perfect served with veggies or chips!"
Stacia Shoults

BEAR BOTTOM BITES

Makes 16 servings

8 large jalapeños

1 bar cream cheese

1 tub cream cheese onion dip

Bear Creek Smokehouse™ Smoked Ham, diced

Bear Creek Smokehouse™ Smoked Bacon, peppered or plain

Halve jalapeño peppers and seed. Soften cream cheese and onion dip then stir together till soft. Stuff jalapeño halves with cream cheese and onion dip mixture. Sprinkle diced ham on top and wrap with Bear Creek Bacon (optional). Bake in 350 degree oven till bacon is sizzling and done... Yummy!

Pâté Of Chicken Livers

Appetizers for 4-6

½ pound chicken livers

1 teaspoon salt

½ teaspoon black pepper

2 Tablespoons melted chicken fat *(not optional)*

1 large yellow or white onion, chopped

2 eggs, hard boiled and peeled

*"Perfect appetizer for an elegant dinner party!
We like to serve it smeared on a fresh baguette!"*
Tracy Shoults

Preheat broiler. Spray cookie pan with non-stick spray. Set aside.

Drain any liquid from the livers and place on the prepared cookie pan. Place the cookie pan under broiler and turn the livers over after 4-5 minutes. Let them remain under the broiler until thoroughly cooked. Let livers cool slightly.

Place livers on a cutting board with the chopped onion. Chop together well. Place liver/onion mixture in medium bowl. Chop eggs and add to mixture along with other ingredients. Cover tightly and refrigerate until well chilled.

Serve as appetizer with crackers or party rye bread.

Fresh Tomato Relish

Makes 8-10 servings

1 bell pepper, finely chopped

1 yellow or white onion, finely chopped

6-8 tomatoes, cored, seeds removed and chopped

½ cup vinegar

⅓ cup water

3 Tablespoons sugar

2 teaspoons salt

½ teaspoon black pepper

In a large bowl, combine all ingredients mixing until well blended. Serve immediately or transfer to a glass bowl. Cover and refrigerate until served.

SPINACH BALLS

Makes 2 Dozen

2 *(10 ounce)* packages frozen chopped spinach

3 cups herb-seasoned stuffing mix

1 large yellow onion, finely chopped

6 eggs, well beaten

¾ cup butter or margarine, melted

½ cup grated parmesan cheese

1 Tablespoon black pepper

1½ teaspoons garlic salt

½ teaspoon dried thyme

Cook spinach according to package directions. Drain in wire mesh strainer. Put spinach in a clean dish towel or cheesecloth. Squeeze to remove excess moisture. Set aside.

Preheat oven to 325 degrees. Spray two cookie sheets with non-stick spray. Set aside.

In a large bowl, combine spinach and remaining ingredients. Mix well. Shape spinach mixture into ¾" balls. (Using a small food scoop will speed this process.) Place Spinach Balls (not touching) on prepared cookie sheets. Bake 15 to 20 minutes. Yields 2 dozen

Note: Spinach balls can be frozen before baking. To freeze, place spinach balls (not touching) on a non-sprayed cookie sheet and freeze. When firm, transfer the spinach balls to a plastic freezer bag and store in the freezer until needed. When ready to cook, place spinach balls (not touching) on a prepared cookie sheet and set at room temperature for a few minutes to allow the spinach balls to thaw slightly. Bake at 325 degrees for 20 to 25 minutes.

From the kitchen of Muriel LaGrone

*...I live by faith in the Son of God,
who loved me and gave himself for me.*

Galatians 2:20

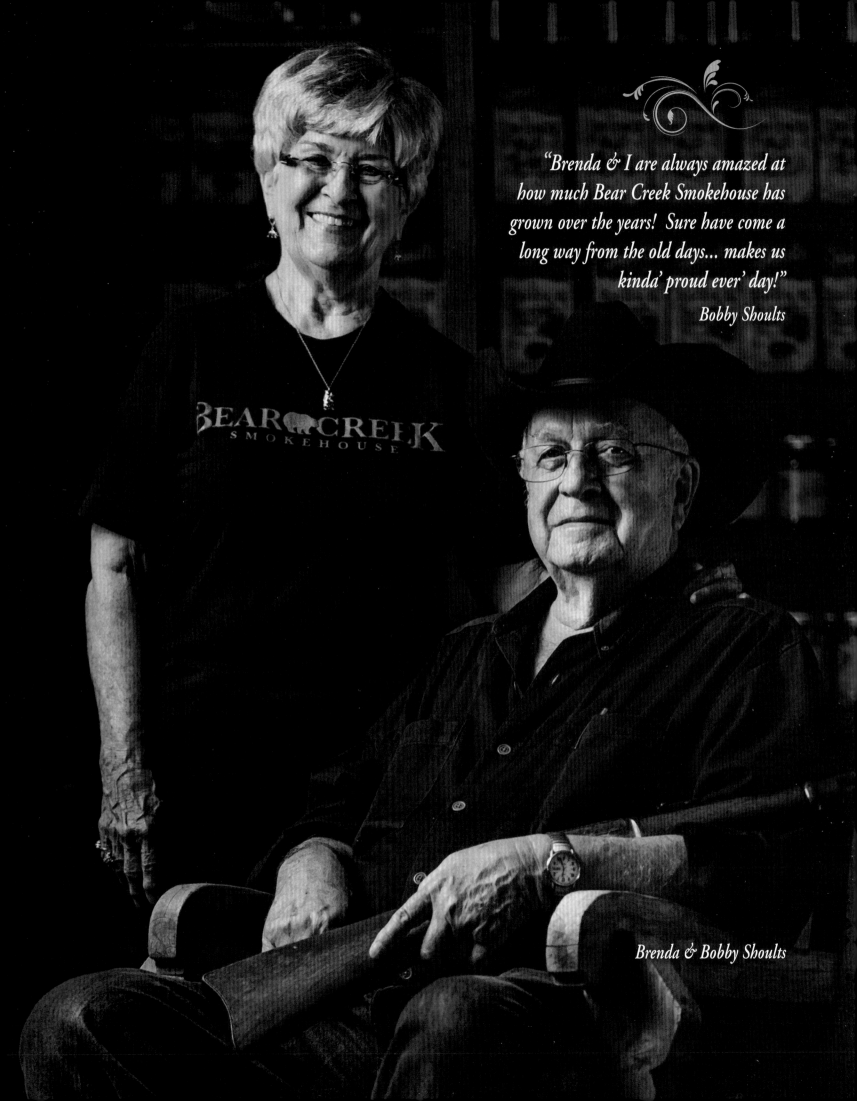

"Brenda & I are always amazed at how much Bear Creek Smokehouse has grown over the years! Sure have come a long way from the old days... makes us kinda' proud ever' day!"

Bobby Shoults

Brenda & Bobby Shoults

PINK DIP

Makes 10-12 servings

16 ounces of your favorite salsa *(we use Albert's)*

8 ounce bar of firm cream cheese

Throw both ingredients in a blender and blend till well mixed. Serve with Fritos® or your favorite corn chips.

From the kitchen of Neina Kennedy

The Salgado Family

- A SPECIAL TRIBUTE TO -
THE SALGADO FAMILY

We would like to pay a special debt of gratitude to The Salgado Family!
They have worked with the Shoults Family for collectively 181 years!

When Robbie was a teenager, he made the trek with Bobby down to Elgin, Texas
to pick up Moises, Armando, their brothers, and wives!

The Shoults Family took them in, gave them jobs, and homes!
Over the years, their wives, in-laws, and children have all worked at the Smokehouse!
Armondo Jr. also received a full scholarship to Texas A&M, and is now a successful Engineer!

Hunter used to play with their kids as a boy... now, his kids play with their grandkids!
We are so glad that they are our neighbors and live here in Bear Bottom!

Bobby, and all of us here at Bear Creek, think of The Salgado's as our extended family!
We are so blessed they have been a part of our lives and success for so many years.
It has been a truly heart-warming story and we love them!
We thank you, from the bottom of our hearts, for your years of dedicated service!

TANGY CHEESE BALL

Appetizers for 12-15

2 *(8 ounce)* packages cream cheese, softened

1½ cups shredded sharp cheddar cheese

1 small yellow onion, minced

2 Tablespoons Worcestershire® sauce

1½ teaspoons minced garlic

1 teaspoon lemon juice

1 cup finely chopped pecans

Combine all ingredients (except pecans) in a large bowl. Mix well.

Form mixture into a ball. Place ball in the refrigerator for at least one hour or until the mixture is chilled and will hold the shape of a ball.

Place the chopped pecans in a flat dish or pan. Roll the chilled cheese mixture gently in the pecans to coat the outside of the ball.

Using a clean piece of plastic wrap, wrap the ball and refrigerate until serving time. Serve with crackers.

"This is a quick, easy solution for an appitizer...
and it's always a hit!"
Tracy Shoults

CUCUMBERS IN VINEGAR

Makes 8-10 servings

¾ cup apple cider vinegar

¼ cup water

¾ cup sugar

1 teaspoon salt

¼ teaspoon pepper

3 cups peeled, sliced cucumbers

In a medium saucepan, bring vinegar, water, and sugar to a boil. Remove from heat and allow the mixture to cool slightly while you are working with the cucumbers.

Place the cucumbers in a glass refrigerator dish. Stir the salt and pepper into the vinegar mixture and pour over the cucumbers. Cover the dish with the cucumbers and refrigerate for one hour. Serve.

...We know that in all things God works for the good of those who love him...

Romans 8:28

Mini Pizzas

Makes 15 servings

1 pound ground beef

1 pound bulk sausage

1 pound Velveeta® cheese, cut into ½" cubes

1 teaspoon ground basil

1 teaspoon ground oregano

¼ teaspoon garlic powder

2 Tablespoons dried parsley flakes

2 loaves party rye bread

"These little Mini Pizzas from Janie are easy-to-make and a perfect quick, appetizer to serve for impromptu guests... always a hit!"
Tracy Shoults

In a large skillet, brown the meats. Drain the drippings from the pan. To the browned meat, add the cheese and stir until melted. Add the basil, oregano, garlic powder, and parsley flakes. Stir to blend the ingredients. Set aside.

Preheat the broiler. Line a cookie sheet with aluminum foil. Set aside.

Lay the bread slices on the prepared cookie sheet in a single layer. Evenly spread the meat mixture over the bread slices. Broil until toasty brown on the tops. Serve immediately.

The mini pizzas can be frozen for later use. To do this, before the broiling step, place the cookie sheet with the prepared pizzas in the freezer. When frozen, the pizzas can be removed from the cookie sheet and carefully placed in freezer bags for later use. When ready to serve, remove the pizzas from the freezer and arrange on a cookie sheet. Broil until toasty brown.

From the kitchen of Janie Watson

- Bear Bottom Tall Tales By Bobby Shoults -

"Each year the shackles that we hang the turkeys by would go through the pit and get stained, so we'd have to stay up at the Smokehouse for hours cleanin' them things! That was a pet peeve... them shackles had to stay clean!"

SADIE'S TEXAS PIZZA

Serves - Varies

Garlic Texas Toast, 2-3 slices per person

Sliced pepperoni

Grated or thinly sliced mozzarella cheese

Marinara sauce or pizza sauce

Your favorite pizza toppings, as desired

Preheat oven to 375 degrees. Cover a baking pan with aluminum foil to eliminate the need for clean-up.

Place the toast slices in a single layer on the prepared pan. Spread a thin layer of sauce evenly over each toast slice. Add pepperoni and your favorite pizza toppings. Cover each piece of toast with cheese. Bake 10-12 minutes or until cheese has completely melted. Serve warm.

"My aunt SaySay makes the best Texas Pizza! She puts extra cheese on mine and I love it!"

Cooper Shoults

Sadie McDonald

DID YOU KNOW?

The smoking of meat and fish has been practiced for ages. Indigenous cultures around the world found that the absorbed smoke acted as a preservative. Perhaps the most famous "smokers of meat" were the Caribbean natives who smoked it on a rack over a smoky fire, a setup they called "barbacoa," an early form of what we know today as barbeque!

GUACAMOLE

Makes 2-4 servings

1 large Hass avocado, pit removed, discard outer skin and cut the flesh into ½" cubes

½ lime, reserve juice from squeezing

2 Tablespoons finely chopped cilantro

¼ teaspoon garlic powder

2 Tablespoons minced jalapeños

2 Tablespoons minced red onion

1 tomato

¼ teaspoon sea salt

¼ teaspoon white pepper

Wash and core the tomato. Cut into thirds and remove seeds. Dice one section of the tomato and put into a medium bowl. Cut the remaining two sections into wedges or chop to use as a garnish. Set aside.

To the bowl, add all remaining ingredients. Mix well. Put the guacamole into a serving dish or plate and garnish with reserved tomato.

From the kitchen of Matt Coleman

CURRY DIP

Makes 2 cups of dip

8 ounces cream cheese, softened

8 ounces sour cream

½ teaspoon dried tarragon

1 teaspoon ground dill

1 teaspoon curry powder

1 teaspoon soy sauce

3 teaspoons lemon juice

Raw vegetables: carrots, cucumbers, cherry tomatoes, bell peppers to dip with

In a bowl, blend cream cheese and sour cream. Add tarragon, dill, curry powder, soy sauce, and lemon juice. Refrigerate until serving time.

Cut carrots, cucumbers, and bell peppers into stick shapes to use for dipping. Cherry tomatoes can be dipped whole. Place dip in a small bowl on the center of the serving plate. Arrange vegetables around the bowl. Serve immediately.

From the kitchen of Becky Shoults Bibb

"Just one of MeMaw's (Nellie's) well worn recipe files! Man, how she could cook!"
Robbie Shoults

AVOCADO SALSA

Makes 4-6 servings

6 Roma tomatoes, seeds removed and diced

1 cup finely chopped red onion

1-2 jalapeños, seeds removed and finely diced

3 medium avocados, diced in ½" cubes

½ cup loosely packed chopped cilantro leaves

3½ Tablespoons olive oil

Juice of 1 lime

1 clove garlic, minced

½ teaspoon salt

¼ teaspoon freshly ground black pepper

In a small mixing bowl, whisk together the olive oil, lime juice, garlic, salt, and pepper. Set aside.

In a large bowl, toss together the tomatoes, onions, jalapeños, cilantro, and avocados. Pour the oil mixture over the vegetables and toss gently to distribute the dressing. Serve immediately with tortilla chips or as a topping for Mexican entrees.

From the kitchen of Tracy Shoults

Tracy Shoults

MARINATED CARROTS

Serves 4-6

5 cups sliced carrots, cut into ¼" slices

1 bell pepper, seeds removed and coarsely chopped

1 onion, coarsely chopped

1 can tomato soup

½ cup vegetable oil

1 cup sugar

1 teaspoon salt

1 teaspoon pepper

1 teaspoon Worcestershire® sauce

In a large saucepan, place carrots with enough water to cover. Bring to full boil. Cook until fork tender. Drain water from the carrots. Add the remaining ingredients and stir well. Put the mixture in a glass or plastic container and refrigerate 12 hours or overnight before serving. Serve chilled or room temperature.

"These carrots are so yummy!
I love eating them after school with my brother!"
Cooper Shoults

"This ole' 'dog trot' cabin, near Bear Bottom, is a stark reminder of the toils & tribulations that our ancestors endured in settlin' this part of Texas!"

Hunter Shoults

FROSTED PEANUTS

Servings 4

1 cup sugar

½ cup water

2 cups raw peanuts

¼ teaspoon ground cinnamon

Preheat oven to 300 degrees. Spray a cookie sheet (with sides) with non-stick spray. Set aside.

Place all ingredients in a large skillet and cook, stirring constantly, over medium-high heat until all liquid has evaporated. Pour the nut mixture onto the prepared cookie sheet. Spread the nuts evenly on the cookie sheet. Bake for 30 minutes. Remove from the oven to cool before storing in an airtight container.

- REMEMBERIN' BEAR BOTTOM BY HUNTER SHOULTS -

"When I was about four years old, Beebee and Poppa got me a second-hand tricycle without a seat! I rode that thing all through the Smokehouse (which USDA wouldn't allow today). I'd ride to the box room and Miss Mattie, who still works in that box room today, would pick me up, set me on the table, and give me a piece of gum. Hard to believe that was over 20 years ago!!"

BEAR BOTTOM BLISS *Salads*

FROZEN FRUIT SALAD

Makes 24 servings

16 ounces whipping cream

1 cup sugar or superfine sugar

½ teaspoon vanilla

8 ounces sour cream

1 Tablespoon fresh lemon juice

1 large can crushed pineapple, drained

8 ounce bottle maraschino cherries, drained and chopped

½ cup chopped pecans

3-4 bananas, diced

24 foil muffin cups

Place the foil muffin cups in 2 muffin tins. Set aside.

In a large mixer bowl, whip the cream. When the cream makes soft peaks, lower the mixer speed and gradually add the sugar. When the cream makes stiff peaks, add the vanilla. Fold in the sour cream and lemon juice. Stir the pineapple, cherries, pecans, and bananas into the whipped cream mixture. Use a large spoon to place the cream mixture evenly in each of the muffin cups. Freeze. After the salads have frozen, cover the trays with foil to prevent freezer burn.

Make these salads a day or two before serving. They transport easily if left in the muffin tins.

From the kitchen of Brenda Shoults

Cooper & Barrett Shoults

MIXED VEGETABLE SALAD

Makes 10-12 servings

1 package frozen green lima beans

1 package frozen cut green beans

1 package frozen English peas

¾ cup mayonnaise

2 hard-boiled eggs, finely grated

½ onion, finely minced

1 teaspoon Worcestershire® sauce

½ teaspoon dry mustard

Juice of ½ lemon

¼ teaspoon garlic salt

¼ teaspoon Tabasco® or your favorite hot sauce

Cook the beans and peas together according to directions on one of the packages. Drain. Put the beans in a large bowl or serving dish. Set aside.

Mix all the remaining ingredients together in a small bowl. Pour the dressing over the vegetables and mix well to coat the beans with the dressing. Serve immediately or cover the dish tightly and refrigerate overnight before serving.

Serve immediately if you prefer to serve it warm... Or refrigerate overnight or a day ahead and serve cold.

From the kitchen of Brenda Shoults

Strawberry Jell-O® Salad

Serves 6

1 *(6 ounce)* box strawberry Jell-O®

2 cups boiling water

1 *(15 ounce)* can crushed pineapple with juice

1 large carton sliced frozen strawberries, thawed

8 ounce package fat free sour cream

Dissolve Jell-O® in boiling water. Add pineapple and strawberries. Pour half of the mixture into serving bowl. Cover with plastic wrap and refrigerate for an hour or until congealed. While mixture is chilling, mix sour cream with the remaining gelatin mixture and set aside on counter top at room temperature. When refrigerated mixture has set up, spread sour cream mixture over the top. Cover with plastic wrap and refrigerate until congealed.

From the kitchen of Charmaine Arnauld

Broccoli Salad

Serves 4-6

2 bunches broccoli

½ pound Bear Creek Smokehouse® bacon, cooked, drained, and crumbled

1 cup finely diced red onion

1 cup raisins

1 cup chopped pecans

1⅓ cups mayonnaise

¼ cup vinegar

¼ cup sugar

Cut broccoli into small florets.

In a large bowl, mix broccoli, bacon, onions, pecans, and raisins. Set aside.

In a small bowl, mix mayo, vinegar, and sugar together. Pour over broccoli mixture. Toss to mix well. Cover and refrigerate until chilled. Serve cold.

From the kitchen of Minnie Wise

"The 'dog trot' cabins were named that due to the fact they had a central breezeway between the two parts of the cabin. This allowed the breeze to cool down the cabin and the dogs, in the hot Texas summers! The foundation was simple and crude... but effective!"

Robbie Shoults

Hot Chicken Salad

Makes 10-12 servings

2 cups cooked, chopped chicken

1½ cups cooked rice

½ cup chopped celery

½ cup chopped bell pepper

½ cup chopped onion

2 hard-boiled eggs, chopped

1 can cream of chicken or cream
of mushroom soup

¾ cup mayonnaise

¼ cup water

1 Tablespoon lemon juice

¾ cup crushed Fritos® or your favorite corn chips

Preheat oven to 375 degrees. Spray a 9" x 13" casserole dish with non-stick spray. Set aside.

In a large bowl, mix together the chicken, rice, celery, onion, bell pepper, and eggs. Set aside.

In another bowl, combine the soup, mayonnaise, water, and lemon juice. Stir to blend the ingredients. Add the soup mixture to the chicken mixture. Stir well. Pour the mixture into the prepared casserole dish. *(The chicken mixture can be covered with plastic wrap and refrigerated overnight at this point, if desired.)* Top with crushed chips and bake for 20-25 minutes or until the top is golden brown and the mixture is bubbly. Serve warm.

From the kitchen of Becky Shoults Bibb

Fresh Apple Salad

Makes 4-6 servings

1½ cups chopped apples

1 cup chopped celery

½ cup raisins

2 Tablespoons mayonnaise

1 Tablespoon sugar

⅛ teaspoon salt

Dash of pepper

In a large bowl, combine apples, celery, and raisins. Set aside.

In a small bowl, combine the mayonnaise, sugar, salt, and pepper. Pour over the apple mixture and toss gently to distribute the dressing evenly. Serve immediately.

LAYERED SALAD

Makes 8-10 servings

1 head leaf or iceberg lettuce, torn into bite size pieces

1 green bell pepper, seeds removed, chopped

½ red onion cut into thin rings

3 ribs of celery, cut into ½" slices

½ pound fresh mushrooms thinly sliced

2 teaspoons lemon juice

1 ¾ cups frozen peas, thawed

2 cups real mayonnaise

1 cup shredded cheddar cheese

5 slices Bear Creek Smokehouse™ bacon, cooked and crumbled

This dish presents well if arranged in a clear glass, upright container. Create layers of ingredients for a pretty presentation. Start by putting the lettuce in the container. Top the lettuce with green pepper and red onion rings. The celery slices are the next layer. Add the mushrooms and sprinkle the lemon juice over the mushrooms. Add the peas in an even layer over the mushrooms. Next add the mayonnaise, evenly covering the vegetables and maneuvering the mayonnaise to touch the container all around the edges. Cover the dish with plastic wrap and refrigerate overnight. Before serving, top the dish with shredded cheese and crumbled bacon.

AVOCADO TOMATO SALAD

Makes 4-6 servings

4 large avocados cut into ½" cubes

1 red onion, finely chopped

1 cup cherry tomatoes cut in halves (or 2 large fresh tomatoes quartered)

⅓ cup olive oil

2 Tablespoons Balsamic vinegar

Salt and pepper to taste

In a small bowl, mix the olive oil, vinegar, salt and pepper. Set aside.

In a large bowl, mix the avocado, onion, and tomatoes. Pour the dressing over the vegetables and toss gently. Serve immediately.

From the kitchen of Tracy Shoults

Orange Jell-O® Salad

Serves 4-6

1 *(15 ounce)* can crushed pineapple

⅔ cup sugar

1 large package orange flavored Jell-O®

2 cups cold water

1 ½ cups grated cheddar cheese

½ cup finely chopped pecans

1 large container of whipped cream, we recommend Cool Whip®, defrosted

In a saucepan over medium heat, stir pineapple (with juice) and sugar until sugar has dissolved. Stir in orange Jell-O®. Add cold water. Refrigerate until the mixture has gelled.

Stir the pineapple/orange gelatin with a fork to break it into small pieces. Add the chopped nuts and grated cheese. Fold in the Cool Whip®. Return the mixture to the refrigerator until congealed. Serve chilled.

From the kitchen of Brenda Shoults

Brenda Shoults

Chicken Salad

Serves 2-4

½ cup mayonnaise

¼ teaspoon garlic powder

¼ teaspoon onion powder

⅛ teaspoon dry mustard

½ cup finely chopped celery

2 Tablespoons finely chopped green onions

1 *(12½ ounce)* can chunk chicken, drained and cut into bite-size pieces

In a small bowl, blend together mayonnaise, garlic powder, onion powder, and mustard. Set aside.

In a medium size bowl, combine celery, chopped green onions, and chicken. Add mayonnaise mixture and toss to evenly distribute dressing. Cover tightly and chill before serving. Store refrigerated.

Walk with the wise and become wise...

Proverbs 13:20

CORN, SPINACH & CHERRY TOMATO SALAD

Serves 6

6-8 large ears corn, shucked

5 slices Bear Creek Smokehouse bacon, cooked, drained, and chopped

2 cups or 12 ounces cherry tomatoes, washed and drained

1 bunch of fresh spinach, stems removed, thoroughly washed and drained

¼ cup finely chopped fresh cilantro, washed and drained

2 cloves garlic, minced

¼ cup fresh lime juice

2 avocados, peeled with pit removed and chopped

Salt and freshly cracked pepper to taste

On a gas or charcoal grill, roast the corn, turning occasionally until just tender and lightly charred. Transfer the corn to a cutting board and let cool. Cut kernels from the corn and place in a large bowl. Add bacon, tomatoes, spinach, cilantro, garlic, avocado, and lime juice. Toss well. Season to taste. Serve immediately.

...Love each other as I have loved you.
...Greater love has no one than this:
to lay down one's life for one's friends.

John 15:12-13

- BEAR BOTTOM TALL TALES BY BOBBY SHOULTS -

"One night the alarm went off in the smokehouse. I jumped into my overalls, threw a suspender over one shoulder, and went to wait for the Sheriff! After a while, I decided to walk through and check everything. I grabbed my shotgun. 'Bout then I saw the Sheriff, so I whistled three times...no response. So I walked back up to the office. Just then I came 'round the corner and ran smack dab into that Sheriff! He said, 'Halt who goes there?'... I said I was the owner. He asked if I had any ID on me. I said 'No, but if you turn around you'll see my picture there on the wall!' I scared that ole boy half to death that night!"

The Bear Creek Gang!

IT'S ALL ABOUT FAITH & FAMILY...

"Family is very important to us here at Bear Creek Smokehouse. That's why we've been able to make the smokehouse last as long as it has. We draw strength from each other" says Robbie Shoults, Vice President of Bear Creek Smokehouse. Robbie's business card declares that he is the 'Head Honcho' in Bear Bottom! He is the third generation of the Shoults family to run the company. "I like to tell folks that on a normal day here, we'll have four generations of our family in the plant at Bear Creek Smokehouse" he says with his signature grin, letting his family pride show!

Bear Creek Smokehouse originally began as an extension of the family farm out in rural Harrison County, Texas. Each of the Shoults boys took their turn in Agriculture Education courses and FFA programs while in high school. There were even a few college classes as well. But the biggest educator for them all has been the school of Bear Creek... first hand, on-the-job training received by experiencing every facet of the business... day in and day out!

The first employees were Fonzo and Stella McKnight. Stella and Nellie Shoults dressed the turkeys in the farm's old wellhouse. In 1947, 'Hick' Shoults built his first smokehouse. It measured 6 by 8 feet and held 30-40 turkeys. It took a day and a half to smoke them and then Fonzo and Hick would deliver them. The next year, he added one twice the size of the original... the following year he added yet another and Bear Creek Smokehouse was in business!

Over the years, countless family members, relatives, and good neighbors have worked at Bear Creek Smokehouse, especially during the fall holiday season. This way the secrets of smoking meats, as well as delicious family recipes, are passed down from one generation to the next. Recipes in this Cookbook are selected from these family recipes!

L-R: Barrett, Hunter, Bobby, Brenda, Cooper Shoults And Krysta Shoults Coleman

The Photo Shoot Team Clockwise: Melissa Yount, Jim Bowie, Cyndi McDonnell, Robbie Shoults, Linda Bellingham, Theo Regas And Chuck Stovall (Not Pictured)

*L-R: Jayson, Mike, Karen, Kim, Hunter, Stacia,
Cooper, Tracy, Barrett And Robbie*

...FIRST, LAST & ALWAYS!

Several Shoults family members currently work for the business, including Robbie's father, Bobby Shoults. Bobby's wife, Brenda, worked in the business office. She filled holiday orders and worked in company sales for many years. Bobby and Brenda managed facility expansions and economic growth of the Bear Creek business from the 1960's into the 1990's, before turning over the reins to son, Robbie. They still keep a close eye on all aspects of Bear Creek. After all, the smokehouse is just a few steps from their house.

Robbie Shoults learned the smokehouse business from his grandparents, Hick and Nellie, and from his parents, Bobby and Brenda. Robbie's wife, Tracy Shoults, also works in the business at Bear Creek. "It's so rewarding to go to work everyday and be with the ones you love, your family," Tracy says. Robbie and Tracy live 'across the pasture' within walking distance to the smokehouse. Robbie has three children that he raised in Bear Bottom. Although his daughters, Krysta and Erin, chose careers outside of Bear Creek Smokehouse, his son, Hunter, decided he wanted to work and carry on his great grandfather's legacy!

Hunter, and his wife, Stacia, have both worked their way up into prominent management roles at the Bear Creek operation. "It always appealed to me," Hunter said. "It's really awesome to me that I get to do the same things that my great-grandfather and grandfather did all their lives, and carry on their traditions. They believed in the company so strongly and ingrained that in me at a young age."

Hunter and Stacia represent the fourth generation of Shoults family members managing Bear Creek Smokehouse. Hunter first began working for his dad at six years old, packing up gift boxes to ship out. After going off to college for a while, he returned to carry on his family's legacy. Now, as a husband and dad with two small children of his own, Hunter runs the smokehouse while Stacia is the office manager.

Everyone at Bear Creek takes pride in the legacy of quality that has been passed down! Of the 40 plus year-round employees at Bear Creek, nine have been here for over 25 years! We're blessed with so many loyal employees in our extended Bear Creek Family!

"Bear Bottom lies in the rugged, natural bottom land, along Bear Creek, in the heart of the East Texas Piney Woods!"
Robbie Shoults

ORIENTAL CHICKEN SALAD

Makes 6-8 servings

6 chicken breasts, cooked and chopped into bite-size pieces

2 bunches of green onions, chopped

¼ cup poppy seeds

¼ cup sugar

¼ cup white vinegar

½ cup vegetable oil

½ teaspoon salt

¼ teaspoon pepper

½ cup slivered almonds

1 can chow mein noodles

In a large bowl, mix the chopped chicken, onions, and poppy seeds. Set aside.

In a small bowl, combine the sugar, vinegar, vegetable oil, salt, and pepper. Pour over the chicken mixture. Stir well to coat all the chicken with the oil mixture. Refrigerate until serving time. Just before serving, stir the almonds and noodles into the chicken mixture.

From the kitchens of Janie Watson and Brenda Shoults

BEAR BOTTOM BLISS

Soups

Spicy Chicken Soup

Serves 8-10

6 chicken breasts

Dash of salt to taste

1 teaspoon garlic powder

1½ Tablespoons onion powder

1 teaspoon pepper

2 Tablespoons dried parsley

5 chicken bouillon cubes

Water

2 Tablespoons olive oil

½ cup chopped onion

1 teaspoon minced garlic

1 jar chunky salsa

1 can peeled, chopped tomatoes

1 can condensed tomato soup

1-2 Tablespoons chili powder

1 can whole kernel corn, drained

1 can black beans, rinsed and drained

1 can navy beans, rinsed and drained

Cayenne pepper to taste

1 *(8 ounce)* sour cream

Handful of shredded cheddar cheese

Place first 8 ingredients in a large kettle. Add enough water to cover the chicken. Bring to simmer and cook until the chicken is cooked through. Turn the heat off and remove the chicken using tongs, and place on a cookie sheet. Let broth sit in kettle, covered. When the chicken is cool enough to work with, shred the meat using two forks. Cover the chicken and set aside.

In a skillet, heat 2 Tablespoons olive oil. Add ½ cup chopped onion and stir until they become translucent. Add minced garlic. Stir well. Add the onion/garlic mixture with remaining ingredients except sour cream and cheese to the kettle.

Stir in shredded chicken. Simmer the soup for 45 minutes to one hour. Taste for seasoning, and add salt and Cayenne pepper if desired. Stir in the 8 ounce container of sour cream. Stir well to blend. Serve immediately with tortilla chips and shredded cheese if desired.

From the kitchen of Stacia Shoults

BROCCOLI CHEESE SOUP

Makes 4-6 servings

½ stick butter

1 package frozen chopped broccoli, finely chopped

1 cup water

1 Tablespoon chicken bouillon granules

1 cup half and half

1 cup Velveeta® cheese cut into ½" cubes

Salt and pepper to taste

In a large saucepan, melt the butter and add broccoli. Add water and chicken bouillon. Bring to a gentle simmer and cook for 20 minutes. Remove the saucepan from the heat. Add half and half and cheese cubes. Stir until cheese has melted and incorporated into the soup. Taste for seasoning and add salt and pepper if needed. Do not allow the soup to boil. Serve warm or at room temperature.

From the kitchen of Nellie Shoults

...Love your enemies, do good to them, and lend to them without expecting to get anything back...

Luke 6:35

*...For everything God created is good,
and nothing is to be rejected if it is
received with thanksgiving...*

1 Timothy 4:4

POTATO SOUP

As seen on pages 53-54. Serves 6-8

4 cups raw potatoes, peeled and diced

1½ cups water

½ cup chopped celery

½ cup chopped onions

1 Tablespoon chicken bouillon granules

1 cup milk

12 ounces sour cream

2 Tablespoons flour

2 teaspoons chopped chives, fresh or freeze dried

Salt and pepper to taste

In a large saucepan, place potatoes in water. Add celery, onions, and bouillon. Simmer for 20 minutes. Add milk. Mix flour with sour cream, stirring until smooth. Add to soup while stirring. Simmer, stirring constantly until slightly thickened. Stir in chives. Taste for seasoning.

From the kitchen of Nellie Shoults

"This is MeMaw's recipe! It is so special to taste something from MeMaw and connect with the past!"
Stacia Shoults

Nellie Shoults

KENNIE'S TACO SOUP

Makes 10-12 servings

2 pounds ground beef

1 large onion, finely chopped

1 package taco seasoning

1 package Hidden Valley® Ranch dip mix

2 cans Ranch Style® beans with Jalapeños

1 can RoTel® tomatoes

1 can stewed tomatoes

Beef stock or broth, as needed

In a large skillet over medium-high heat, sauté the ground beef while breaking it up into small pieces. When the beef has browned, add the onions and continue cooking until the onions are translucent. Stir in the taco seasoning and dip mix. Add the beans and tomatoes. Lower the heat to the lowest setting and cover the skillet. Allow to simmer for 1½ hours. Stir the soup occasionally during the cooking time. Add beef stock if needed to reach the desired consistency. Serve warm.

Cheesy Chicken Soup

Makes 6-8 servings

1 whole chicken

3 stalks celery, cut into ½" slices

1 onion, finely chopped

1 cup long grain rice

1 cup Velveeta® cheese cut into ½" cubes

Salt and pepper, to taste

Give thanks to the Lord, for he is good;
his love endures forever.

1 Chronicles 16:34

Place chicken in a large stock pot. Add enough water to cover the chicken. Place over medium heat and bring to a simmer. Cook until the chicken is tender and falling off the bone. Carefully remove the chicken from the pot onto a large platter to cool slightly. To the pot, add the celery, onion, and rice. Lower the heat and allow to cook while you work with the chicken. Remove the skin and bones from the chicken. Tear or cut the chicken into bite size pieces. Set aside.

Taste the chicken stock for seasoning. Add salt and pepper if needed. When the rice is tender, add the cheese cubes and chicken. Turn off the heat, and stir the soup until the cheese has melted. Serve warm.

From the kitchen of Kennie Smith

- Bear Bottom Tall Tales By Bobby Shoults -

"Back in the day, when we used to raise pigs, one year it was the coldest winter we'd had 'round these parts for years. I went out one night to stoke up the heat in the barn so the pigs wouldn't freeze overnight. Well, I look down and notice that the new brood of piglets are already turnin' blue from the cold! So I threw those little critters in a box and took 'em in to set by the fire to warm up and I went on to bed.

Middle of the night I wake up to Brenda pokin' me sayin' that somethin' was runnin' around the house! Sure 'nough those little piglets had warmed up and come back to life, and were runnin' 'round squeelin' and tearin'-up-jack! That was one crazy night!"

VEGETABLE BEEF SOUP

Makes 8-10 servings

1½ to 2 pounds lean ground beef

1 onion, chopped

1 Tablespoon flour

32 ounces beef broth *(plus more if needed)*

3 cups potatoes, peeled and cut into ½" cubes

¼ head cabbage, chopped very fine

1 can cut green beans, drained

1 can whole kernel corn, drained

In a large kettle, brown the beef breaking the meat into small pieces. Cook until the beef has browned. Add the onions and cook until the onions are translucent. Stir in the flour and mix well. Add the beef broth and the potatoes. Heat over medium-low heat, stirring the soup occasionally until it reaches a simmer. Cover the kettle and cook the soup until the potatoes test done. To test, stick a fork into one, if the potato slides off the fork with ease, they are ready. Add green beans, corn, and cabbage. If more liquid is needed to reach a soup consistency, add more beef broth. Heat until the mixture simmers again. Serve warm.

POTATO SOUP

Makes 8-10 servings

6 large potatoes, peeled and cut into ½" cubes

4 Tablespoons butter

1 large onion, finely chopped

Water, as needed

4 carrots, cleaned and thinly sliced

1 can cream of mushroom soup

1 pound Velveeta® cheese, cut into ½" cubes

Chicken stock, if needed

Salt and pepper to taste

In a large saucepan or kettle, melt butter. Stir in potatoes, carrots, and onions. Cook for about five minutes or until onions become translucent. Add enough water to the pot to cover the vegetables. Add mushroom soup. Simmer until potatoes are softened. Mash with a potato masher. If the soup is too thick, add enough chicken stock to reach the desired consistency. Add the cheese cubes and stir until melted. Remove from heat. Taste the soup for seasonings and add salt and/or pepper to taste.

From the kitchen of Tracy Shoults

BEAR BOTTOM BLISS *Breads*

Jalapeño Cheese Puffs

Serves 12

8 ounces cheddar cheese, grated

8 ounces Monterrey Jack cheese, grated

½ cup half and half

4 eggs

3 Tablespoons flour

2 teaspoons baking powder

Sliced jalapeños, to taste

8 ounces Bear Creek Smokehouse™ cooked ham, bacon or sausage, chopped *(optional)*

Preheat oven to 325 degrees.

Spray 9" x 13" baking pan with non-stick spray. Set aside.

Put both the cheddar and Monterrey jack cheese in a large zip plastic bag. Add flour and baking powder to the bag and zip shut. Shake the bag to evenly coat the cheese with dry ingredients. Layer the cheese mixture and jalapeños in the prepared baking pan. If you are using the optional meats, layer them with the cheese and jalapeños. Set aside.

In a large bowl, mix the half and half and eggs with a fork or whisk until well blended. Pour over ingredients in the baking pan.

Bake for 30-35 minutes or until set and lightly browned on top. Let cool slightly. Cut into serving-size squares.

From the kitchen of Muriel LaGrone

"It was always a special treat when Muriel made these savory Jalapeño Cheese Puffs for us kids... we would always come back for more... every time!"
Tracy Shoults

DELICIOUS CORNBREAD DRESSING

Serves 12

5 boxes cornbread mix, prepared according to directions, cooled to room temperature and crumbled

12 hamburger buns, toasted and crumbled

1 cup finely chopped onion

4 green onions, tops and bulbs chopped

½ cup chopped celery leaves

4 large eggs, hard boiled and diced

1 quart stock from baked turkey or chicken stock

Salt and pepper to taste

Preheat oven to 400 degrees.

Spray large 9" x 13" casserole dish with non-stick spray. Set aside.

In a large bowl, combine all ingredients except stock. Using a large spoon, gently toss to mix well.

Drizzle ¼ of the stock into the bread mixture. Toss to distribute the liquids.

Keep the dressing as fluffy as possible. Continue adding stock and mixing dressing until liquid is evenly incorporated into the dressing.

Pour dressing into the baking sheet and gently spread to cover pan evenly.

Place in oven for 12-15 minutes.

Remove from oven. With a large spoon or spatula, turn the dressing mixture to expose moist dressing.

Return to oven for 12-15 minutes longer or until top of dressing is golden brown. Serve warm.

From the kitchen of Nellie Shoults

DID YOU KNOW?

The event that Americans commonly call the "First Thanksgiving" was celebrated by the Pilgrims after their first harvest in the New World in 1621. This feast lasted three days, and as accounted by attendee Edward Winslow, it was attended by 90 Native Americans and 53 Pilgrims! Cornbread Dressing has become a traditional staple at any Thanksgiving feast!

YAYA'S MONKEY BREAD

Serves 6-8

Hunter Shoults, Kim Shoults,
Erin Shoults Marino & Krysta Shoults Coleman

3 cans biscuits

2 sticks butter, melted

1 cup sugar

5 teaspoons cinnamon

Chopped pecans *(optional)*

Preheat oven to 400 degrees.

Spray a 9" x 13" baking pan or a bunt cake pan with non-stick spray. If you are using chopped pecans, distribute them evenly over the bottom of the pan. Set aside.

With a sharp knife or kitchen scissors, cut each biscuit into quarters. Place biscuit portions in the bottom of the prepared baking dish. Set aside.

In a small bowl, mix the melted butter, sugar, and cinnamon. Drizzle mixture evenly over biscuits.

Bake for 20 minutes or until golden brown.

From the kitchen of Kim Shoults

"Me and my sisters,
Erin & Krysta, always loved
it when Mom would make us
this special delicious treat!"
Hunter Shoults

VONDELL'S YEAST ROLLS

Makes approximately 2 dozen rolls

4 cups self-rising flour

⅔ cup vegetable oil

1 package dry yeast

2 cups warm water

¼ cup sugar

1 egg

Spray two muffin tin pans with non-stick spray. Set aside.

In a large mixing bowl, add yeast to the warm water and stir to dissolve. Stir in sugar. Add oil and egg, mixing until well combined. One cup at a time, stir in the flour, mixing well after each addition. Spoon the mixture evenly into the prepared muffin tins. Set aside for one hour for the batter to rise. Preheat oven to 400 degrees. Bake the rolls until golden brown.

"The old grain elevators in Marshall, Texas, have been deserted for decades... but I can still remember coming here as a kid, with my dad, wishing I could go exploring inside!"

Robbie Shoults

REFRIGERATOR ROLLS

¾ cup solid shortening

¾ cup sugar

1½ teaspoons salt

1 cup water, boiling

2 packages dry yeast

1 cup water, luke warm

2 eggs, well beaten

6 cups flour

"We consider these rolls 'Divinely Inspired'... probably because we always came home from church on Sundays to their intoxicating aroma filling the house!"
Brenda Shoults

In a large bowl, mix shortening, sugar, salt and boiling water. Set aside to cool.

In another large bowl, combine yeast with warm water. Stir well.

Add eggs to the shortening mixture and mix to combine. Add shortening mixture to yeast mixture. Add flour, one cup at a time, mixing well after each addition of flour. Turn dough into a large, lightly oiled bowl. Cover with plastic wrap. Store dough in refrigerator until needed. Dough will keep 7-10 days covered in the refrigerator.

When ready to bake, form rolls and place on lightly oiled baking pan or muffin tin. Cover loosely with clean towel and set aside in draft-free, warm area until doubled in size. When rolls have risen to desired size, preheat oven to 425 degrees. Bake rolls 12-15 minutes or until golden brown.

SQUASH MUFFINS

Serves 4-6

2 cups flour

1 Tablespoon baking powder

¼ teaspoon salt

2 Tablespoons sugar

⅔ cup grated yellow squash

1 egg

¾ cup milk

2 Tablespoons vegetable oil

Preheat oven to 350 degrees. Spray muffin tins with non-stick spray. If you choose to use paper liners, place them in the cups. Set aside.

In a large bowl, combine flour, baking powder, salt, and sugar. Set aside.

In another bowl, combine remaining ingredients and mix well. Stir liquid ingredients into large bowl with dry ingredients. Stir until dry ingredients are moistened. Spoon batter into reserved muffin tins, filling each muffin cup two-thirds full. Bake 20-25 minutes or until lightly browned. Remove from oven and place the muffins on a wire rack to cool.

From the kitchen of Laurie Stacy

"These lightly sweet muffins are both tasty and nutritious... great for breakfast or snacking anytime!"
Laurie Stacy

*"We love to watch our Longhorns and they love watchin'
us back! The kids just love their big 'ole long horns!"*

Hunter Shoults

ZUCCHINI BREAD

Serves 16 slices

3 cups flour

1 teaspoon salt

1 teaspoon baking soda

1 teaspoon baking powder

2 teaspoons ground cinnamon

½ teaspoon ground or finely grated nutmeg

¼ teaspoon ground cloves

2 cups sugar

1 cup chopped pecans or walnuts

3 eggs

2 cups grated zucchini

1 (8 ounce) can crushed pineapple, drained

1 cup vegetable oil

2 teaspoons vanilla

Preheat oven to 325 degrees. Grease and flour two loaf pans. Set aside.

In a large bowl, sift the first eight ingredients. Set aside.

In a large mixing bowl, beat eggs until foamy. Stir in zucchini, pineapple, oil, and vanilla.

Add flour mixture, one cup at a time, to egg mixture. Stir with a spatula until blended. Fold in chopped nuts. Evenly divide batter into the loaf pans. Bake 35-40 minutes or until bread is golden brown. Remove from oven to wire racks. Let cool for 10 minutes before removing breads from the pans. Continue cooling loaves until they reach room temperature before slicing.

From the kitchen of Mary Ann

HUSH PUPPIES

Makes approximately 20

1 cup cornmeal

¾ cup flour

1 teaspoon baking soda

½ teaspoon salt

1 cup buttermilk

Vegetable oil for frying

Preheat oil to 375 degrees. Line a cookie sheet with several layers of paper towels. Set aside. In a large bowl, mix cornmeal, flour, baking soda, and salt. Stir in buttermilk and mix until dry ingredients are blended. To form hush puppies, place a heaping tablespoonful of the batter into your palm and gently squeeze into an elongated ball. Carefully add the batter to the oil. Cook only five or six hush puppies at one time. When the hush puppies reach golden brown on both sides, remove from the oil with a slotted spoon. Place the hush puppies on the paper towel lined cookie sheet while you continue frying the remaining batter. Continue until all batter has been fried.

"These hush puppies are sooo good! They remind me of summer lake days with my brothers!"
Stacia Shoults

CHEESE BREAD

Serves 4-6

1 loaf French bread, sliced in half horizontally

1 small can chopped black olives, drained

1 bunch green onions, chopped finely

3 cups shredded cheddar cheese

1 cup mayonnaise

1 cup finely chopped Bear Creek Smokehouse™ ham *(optional)*

Preheat oven to 350 degrees. Cover a cookie sheet with aluminum foil. Set aside.

Separate bread halves and lay each half with cut side facing up on the prepared cookie sheet. Spread mayonnaise evenly over the cut surfaces. Distribute the olives and green onions *(also ham, if you choose)* evenly over the top. Distribute the shredded cheese evenly over the bread halves. Bake the bread for 15-20 minutes or until the cheese is hot and bubbly.

From the kitchen of Anita Overhultz

BRAN MUFFINS

Makes 24 muffins

1½ cups bran cereal, we recommend All Bran® cereal

1½ cups raisin bran cereal

1 cup boiling water

2 eggs

2 cups buttermilk

½ cup vegetable oil

2 cups honey

1 cup chopped walnuts or pecans

1 cup raisins

2½ teaspoons soda

½ teaspoon salt

2½ cups whole-wheat flour

24 muffin cup liners

Preheat oven to 400 degrees. Place muffin cup liners into two muffin tin trays. Spray each cup with non-stick spray. Set aside.

In a large bowl, mix the two cereals with boiling water. Set aside.

In another large bowl, mix eggs, buttermilk, oil, and honey. Stir in the nuts, raisins, and cereal mixture. Set aside.

Combine the flour, soda, and salt. Stir into the cereal mixture until the dry ingredients are just moistened. Spoon the batter evenly into the prepared muffin cups. Bake 20-25 minutes or until the tops are golden brown. Let cool before serving or storing.

From the kitchen of Anita Overhultz

Anita Overhultz

"These bran muffins are perfect for breakfast and an excellent source of fiber!"
Brenda Shoults

"My Dad used to take me to the Marshall Barber Shop for haircuts. He would promise me that if I behaved, we'd go get ice cream in town! I ALWAYS behaved!"

Robbie Shoults

CRAWFISH CORNBREAD

Serves 12

1 package cornbread mix

1 pound shelled crawfish, fresh
or frozen *(do not drain)*

3 eggs

½ cup chopped onion

½ cup chopped bell pepper

½ cup chopped green onion, tops and bulbs

2 jalapeño peppers, seeds removed and chopped

1 stick butter, melted

2 cups grated cheese

1 can cream corn

1 teaspoon baking soda

1 teaspoon salt

1 teaspoon creole seasoning

Preheat oven to 350 degrees.

Spray a 9" x 13" baking dish with non-stick spray.
Set aside.

In a large bowl, mix all ingredients together until
blended.

Pour batter into prepared baking dish. Bake 45-60
minutes or until set and top is lightly browned.

From the kitchen of Tracy Shoults

Casual
Entertainment

Bear Bottom Breakfast Casserole

Serves 12

16 ounces Monterrey Jack/
Cheddar cheese blend, grated

3 Tablespoons all-purpose flour

2 teaspoons baking powder

1 cup half and half

8 eggs

8 ounces Bear Creek Smokehouse™
Smoked Ham, diced

1 cup finely chopped red onion

1 red bell pepper, seeds removed
and finely chopped

1 *(7 ounce)* can, sliced jalapeños, drained

"This casserole is easy-to-make and is always a popular treat with everyone here in Bear Bottom! Just seems to get the day started off right!"
Brenda Shoults

Preheat oven to 325 degrees. Spray 9"x 12" casserole dish with non-stick cooking spray. Set aside.

Put grated cheese in gallon size food storage bag. Add flour and baking powder. Close bag and shake well. Set aside.

Beat eggs with wire whisk in large bowl. Add half and half and mix well. Set aside.

In a large bowl, mix ham, onion, bell pepper, and jalapeños.

Place ½ of the ham mixture in the prepared casserole dish. Sprinkle ½ of the cheese evenly into the casserole over ham. Add remaining ham and top with remaining cheese mixture. Pour egg mixture over ingredients in casserole dish. Bake for 35-40 minutes, until mixture is set and slightly golden on top. Serve warm.

Optional: Cooked, drained, and crumbled bacon or breakfast sausage may be used in place of ham. Also optional: fresh sliced jalapeños can be used as a garnish.

Did You Know?

Your Mother was actually right... Breakfast IS the most important meal of the day! Studies show that eating a balanced breakfast can give you improved concentration and better performance all throughout the day. A balanced breakfast is also linked to weight control, strength, endurance, and lower cholesterol levels. We know it's a favorite here in Bear Bottom!

Beef Enchiladas

Serves 4-6

4 to 5 teaspoons chili powder

2 teaspoons salt

½ teaspoon ground cumin

2 cloves garlic, minced

3½ cups water

2 *(6 ounce)* cans tomato paste

1 dash Tabasco or other pepper sauce

Oil

12 corn tortillas

1 to 1½ pounds lean ground beef

1 medium onion, chopped

2 cups shredded cheddar cheese, divided

½ cup sliced or chopped black olives

"There's nothin' quite like sittin' down to eat a big plate of beef enchiladas... all smothered in melted cheese! These are some of the best I've had!"
Hunter Shoults

Preheat oven to 350 degrees. Spray a 9"x 13" baking pan with non-stick oil. Set aside.

In a medium saucepan, combine first seven ingredients. Simmer 20 minutes. Set aside.

In a medium skillet with ½" oil, fry tortillas one at a time until softened. This will take only a few seconds on each side. Remove tortillas to drain on paper towels. Set aside.

In a large skillet over medium heat, brown beef. Drain excess fat. Stir chopped onions into beef. Cook, stirring often, until onions are translucent. Remove pan from heat. Add one cup cheese, one cup of the tomato paste mixture, and olives.

Pour remaining tomato paste mixture into prepared baking pan. Place one tortilla on a kitchen work surface. Spoon a heaping tablespoon of the beef mixture down the center of the tortilla. Fold or roll the tortilla around filling and place seam side down in the baking dish. Repeat with all tortillas. Pour any remaining beef mixture over tortillas in baking pan. Sprinkle with remaining cheese. Bake uncovered for 20 to 25 minutes or until hot and bubbly.

Did You Know?

Tex-Mex is a term describing a fusion of American and Mexican cuisine. It derives its name from culinary creations of Tejanos, and has spread from border states, like Texas, to the rest of the country!

Chicken & Broccoli

Serves 4-6

4 carrots, cleaned and cut into ⅛" slices

1 large onion, diced

3 stalks celery, diced

½ cup chicken stock

Salt

Lemon pepper

1 chicken, cooked, de-boned and cut into bite size pieces

2 cans cream of mushroom soup

2 *(8 ounce)* cartons sour cream

2 *(10 ounce)* packages frozen chopped broccoli

8 ounces cheddar cheese, grated

½ cup slivered almonds

2 cups cooked rice

Preheat oven to 350 degrees. Spray a 2 quart casserole dish with non-stick spray. Set aside.

In a large saucepan, cook carrots, onion, and celery in chicken stock until tender, adding water if necessary. Add chicken. Season with salt and lemon pepper to taste. Set aside.

In a medium bowl, combine soup and sour cream. Set aside.

Layer chicken, rice, broccoli, soup mixture and cheese in a prepared casserole dish. Bake for 45 minutes. Remove from oven, sprinkle with almonds, and return to oven for 10 minutes.

Serve immediately. Great served with warm cornbread and butter.

"This is one of my favorite Chicken & Broccoli recipes! It also adds a festive touch of color to any table!"
Tracy Shoults

RED BEANS & RICE

Serves 10-12

1 pound dried red beans

½ pound Bear Creek Smokehouse™ Salt Pork, cut into 1" cubes

3 cups chopped onions

1 cup chopped green onions

1 cup chopped parsley leaves

1 Tablespoon garlic salt

¼ teaspoon dried oregano

1 teaspoon red pepper flakes or cayenne

1 Tablespoon Worcestershire

1 teaspoon ground black pepper

1½ teaspoons hot sauce

1 *(8 ounce)* can tomato sauce

1 pound Bear Creek Smokehouse™ Smoked Sausage or cajun-style sausage, cut into 1" pieces

Long grain white rice prepared according to package directions

The day before serving, sort and wash beans. Place in a large pot and cover with water. Bring water 2" above beans. Cover pot and soak overnight. The next day, drain soaked water. Add water and Bear Creek Smokehouse™ Salt Pork to the pot. Bring to a simmer. Cover and cook for 45 minutes. Add onions, parsley, garlic salt, oregano, red pepper flakes or cayenne, Worcestershire sauce, black pepper, hot sauce, and tomato sauce. Simmer for one hour. While the bean mixture simmers, brown sausage in a skillet. Add Bear Creek Smokehouse™ Sausage to beans. Cook beans for another 30-45 minutes. Add water to beans if needed.

To serve, place large spoon of cooked rice in serving dish. Top rice with beans.

"This is pretty much a staple around here in Bear Bottom! It's especially good served with cornbread and butter, on a cold winter day"
Tracy Shoults

- BEAR BOTTOM TALL TALES BY BOBBY SHOULTS -

"One time I took Brenda out to check the water in the turkey troughs. I had to run back inside and told her I'd be right back. While I was gone, those turkeys just swarmed all over her! She was a'yellin' and a'kickin' at 'em, makin' it all worse!

Them turkeys didn't want any part o'her... last time I ever asked her to check the troughs!"

Green Bean, Bacon & Squash Casserole

Serves 12

1 pound fresh or frozen green beans *(ends trimmed)*

1 pound squash, julienned *(combine your favorite squash varieties)*

1 pound Bear Creek Smokehouse™ Smoked Bacon

1 cup finely chopped red bell pepper, seeds removed

1 cup finely chopped red onion

½ cup butter

½ cup all-purpose flour

3 pints heavy cream

Salt and black pepper

1½ cups grated cheddar/jack cheese blend

Preheat oven to 350 degrees. Spray 9" x 13" casserole dish with non-stick spray. Set aside.

Fill a large stock pot halfway with water and bring to a boil. Meanwhile, fill a large bowl with ice and water. Set the ice-filled bowl in a clean, empty sink. Nestle a colander into the bowl with ice water. Blanch green beans in the boiling water for one minute. Remove with a slotted spoon or tongs to the colander. Blanch squash in the boiling water for one minute. Remove to colander to cool, adding more ice to the bowl if necessary. When vegetables have cooled, remove the colander from the water to allow the vegetables to drain. Set aside.

Pan fry bacon. When bacon is almost crisp, add onion and red bell pepper. Stir occasionally until onion is translucent. Drain bacon drippings from the mixture. Spread ½ bacon/onion mixture in bottom of prepared casserole dish. Layer green beans and squash on top of bacon mixture. Top with remaining ½ bacon/onion mixture. Set aside.

In a large saucepan, melt butter. Whisk flour into the melted butter and cook for two minutes, stirring constantly. Add cream slowly while whisking and cook until sauce thickens. Pour sauce over green beans in casserole dish. Pepper generously over sauce and add salt if desired. Top with cheese. Bake for 25 minutes or until cheese has melted and sauce is bubbling. Serve warm.

JAMBALAYA

Serves 6-8

¼ cup vegetable oil or bacon drippings

1 chicken, cut into pieces or de-boned and cut into serving size pieces

1½ pounds cajun-style sausage, sliced into 1" pieces

4 cups chopped onions

2 cups chopped celery

2 cups chopped green peppers, seeds removed

1 Tablespoon minced garlic

4 cups long grain rice

5 cups chicken stock

Salt

Cayenne pepper

2 cups chopped green onions

In a kettle or stock pot, brown chicken in oil or drippings over medium-high heat. Add sausage and sauté briefly with chicken. Using slotted spoon, remove meats from the pot. Set aside.

Add onions, celery, and green pepper to the pot. Stir often while cooking. When vegetables are lightly browned, add garlic. Stir well. Return meats to the kettle and add stock. Add rice and bring to a simmer. Cover kettle and reduce heat. Cook for 30 minutes, checking pot and stirring well every 10 minutes. Taste to adjust seasoning. Serve warm.

Top each serving with a sprinkling of green onions.

CHEESY BROCCOLI CHICKEN SURPRISE

Serves 4-6

4 boneless, skinless chicken breasts

1 can cheddar cheese soup

1 can cream of chicken soup

1 can chicken broth

¼ cup shredded cheddar

1 tablespoon seasoned salt

1 teaspoon ground pepper

1 large bunch of chopped steamed broccoli or a bag frozen chopped broccoli *(thawed)*

1 *(8 ounce)* container of sour cream

Place first seven ingredients in a slow cooker, cover and cook on high for four hours; or on low for six hours.

Remove chicken breasts and place on a cutting board.

Chop the chicken and return to the slow cooker.

Cover the slow cooker and cook 10 minutes. Stir in the whole container of sour cream.

Add steamed broccoli 10 minutes before serving.

Serve over cooked white rice.

From the kitchen of 'Cupcake' Shoults

- REMEMBERIN' BEAR BOTTOM BY HUNTER SHOULTS -

"Goin' fishin' with Dad & Poppa was always an adventure! Every summer a few of us would go fishin' on the Mississippi River, we'd fish all day, and go frog giggin' at night!

Well, one night the frog gig pole broke in half, and 'ol Bill Whyte, a friend of ours we'd brought along, up and decided he'd just jump in and catch them frogs... only the water was deeper than he thought, and he sank like a rock!

Can't remember if we got any frogs that night... but we all laughed so loud and hard, we probably scared 'em all away anyway!"

CHICKEN SPAGHETTI

Serves 12

1 whole chicken

2 teaspoons salt

2 boxes spaghetti, broken into 3-4" pieces

2 tablespoons olive oil

1 large onion, chopped

2 bell peppers, seeds removed and chopped

4 cloves garlic, minced

1 *(15 ounce)* can crushed tomatoes

1 *(15 ounce)* can tomato sauce

2 tablespoons Worcestershire

Hot pepper sauce, to taste

1 can cream of mushroom soup

12 ounces monterrey jack cheese, grated

"We all love it when BeeBee (Brenda) makes her Chicken Spaghetti! It's definitely a staple at family suppers!"
Hunter Shoults

In a large kettle, cover chicken with water. Add two teaspoons of salt. Simmer until tender. Remove chicken to a large plate to cool. Return kettle to heat and bring to a boil. Cook spaghetti in the chicken stock until tender. Drain spaghetti and set aside. When chicken has cooled enough to handle, remove bones and chop the meat into bite-size pieces. Mix chicken meat with cooked spaghetti in a large bowl. Set aside.

Preheat oven to 350 degrees. Spray a large casserole dish with non-stick spray. Set aside.

In a large skillet, sauté onion and peppers in olive oil until tender. Stir in minced garlic, tomatoes, tomato sauce, soup, and remaining seasonings. Stir mixture into spaghetti/chicken. Place one half of the mixture in prepared casserole dish. Top with half the cheese. Add remaining spaghetti mixture and top with remaining cheese. Bake 30-40 minutes or until mixture is hot and bubbly and the cheese has melted.

From the kitchen of Brenda Shoults

...Love is patient, love is kind. It does not envy, it does not boast, it is not proud. It does not dishonor others, it is not self-seeking, it is not easily angered, it keeps no record of wrongs. Love does not delight in evil but rejoices with the truth...

1 Corinthians 13:4-7

CREOLE SHRIMP SKILLET

As seen on pages 76-77. Makes 2-4 servings

2 Tablespoons olive oil

½ cup finely chopped onion

½ cup celery, cut into ½" pieces

½ cup green pepper, seeds discarded and finely chopped

2 cloves garlic, finely minced

2 cups canned tomatoes, crushed or chopped

¼ teaspoon hot pepper sauce

1 teaspoon dried basil

½ teaspoon dried oregano

2-4 ounces rice

8-10 ounces shrimp, shelled and de veined

Put the olive oil into a large skillet over medium-high heat. Add onion, celery, and green pepper. Cook while stirring until the onions are translucent. Add the garlic. Stir well. Add tomatoes, hot sauce, basil, oregano, and rice. Stir to blend. Reduce the heat to low and cover the skillet. Simmer gently for 10 minutes. Arrange the shrimp on top of the mixture. Cover the skillet and cook an additional 10 minutes. Serve warm.

Turn from evil and do good;
seek peace and pursue it.

Psalm 34:14

STRING BEAN CASSEROLE

Makes 6-8 servings

1 pound lean ground meat

1 onion, chopped

1 egg

¾ teaspoon salt

1 *(16 ounce)* can green beans, drained

1 can mushroom soup

Pepper to taste

Preheat oven to 350 degrees. Spray a casserole dish with non-stick spray. Set aside.

In a large bowl, mix all ingredients to blend well. Put mixture in the prepared pan. Bake 45 minutes or until meat is cooked throughout.

From the kitchen of Twinkle Ryan

BILL DORSEY'S CASSEROLE

Serves 12

1 pound lean ground meat

1 can Spanish rice

1 can Ranch Style® beans, drained

1 can Rotel® tomatoes

1 can whole kernel corn, drained

1 packet cornbread mix, mixed according to package instructions but not cooked/baked

Preheat oven to 350 degrees. Spray a 9" x 13" casserole dish with non-stick spray. Set aside.

In a large skillet, brown the ground meat. Drain off pan juices if desired. To the meat, add Spanish rice, beans, corn, and RoTel® tomatoes. Stir to blend all ingredients. Pour the mixture into the prepared casserole dish and spread evenly in the pan. Pour the prepared cornbread batter evenly over the meat mixture. Bake 25-30 minutes or until the corn bread is lightly browned and the meat mixture is bubbly.

"Bill Dorsey was my uncle... I called him 'Uncle Billy.' He and I used to work together at the Holiday Gift Shows. He was quite a beloved character, telling tall tales and flirtin'! All these years later, I still have people ask me about Uncle Billy!"

Robbie Shoults

SMOKED HAM, MAC & CHEESE

Serves 10-12

1 pound elbow macaroni, cooked according to package directions; drained

1 pound Velveeta® cheese, cut into ½" cubes

1 can cheese soup

1 cup shredded cheddar cheese

1 can evaporated milk

1 cup diced Bear Creek Smokehouse® ham

1 sleeve round buttered crackers, we recommend Ritz® crackers

Pepper

1 stick butter,

Preheat oven to 350 degrees. Spray a 9" x 13" casserole dish with non-stick spray. Set aside.

In a large bowl, combine macaroni, cheese cubes, evaporated milk, shredded cheese, and ham. Add soup to macaroni mixture. Pour mixture into prepared casserole dish. Set aside.

Place crackers in a heavy weight food storage bag. Gently crush crackers by rolling with a rolling pin. Add warm melted butter to the bag and close bag tightly. Rock the bag from side-to-side to coat crumbs with butter. Distribute cracker crumbs evenly over top of macaroni mixture. Bake uncovered for 30 minutes or until crackers are golden and casserole is bubbly. Serve warm.

From the kitchen of Annette Rawson

"This recipe has become one of the best sides in our catering business and is requested time after time from our customers!"

Robbie Shoults

DID YOU KNOW?

The Bear Creek Smoked Ham is hand-cured and smoked in a time-honored process that takes a full five days to complete! After a unique hand preparation of the meat, it is then slowly smoked over Hickory embers until fully-cooked to achieve its signature smoked perfection!

ZESTY BLACK BEAN CHICKEN

Serves 2-3

1 cup frozen corn kernels or 1 can corn, drained

1 can black beans, rinsed and drained

1 jar salsa

1 cup chicken broth

1 Tablespoon taco seasoning

½ teaspoon oregano

2 boneless, skinless chicken breasts

2 cups cooked white rice

1 cup chopped green onions for garnish

Preheat oven to 350 degrees. Spray a baking dish with non-stick spray. Spread the rice over the bottom of the pan. Arrange the chicken breasts side by side on the rice. Set aside.

In a mixing bowl, combine remaining ingredients. Stir to blend. Pour the mixture over rice and top with shredded cheddar cheese. Bake 30-40 minutes.

To serve, sprinkle ¼ cup chopped green onions over each portion.

"This part of East Texas is dotted with old relics, often in and around the old abandoned barns, like my dad used to play in as a kid!"

Hunter Shoults

Cabbage Tamales

Makes 8-10 servings

1½ pounds cooked ground beef, pork or turkey *(or combination)*

1 small yellow or white onion, finely chopped

½ cup rice, uncooked

Salt and pepper to taste

1 head of cabbage, leaves separated

Tomato juice

Bacon drippings, optional

"This Cabbage Tamale recipe of Juanice's is a nice change-of-pace treat and a family favorite!"
Stacia Shoults

Preheat oven to 325 degrees. Spray a 9" x 13" glass baking dish with non-stick spray. Set aside.

In a large bowl, mix cooked ground meat, onion, and rice. Season the mixture with salt and pepper to your taste. Stir well. Using one cabbage leaf at a time, place a heaping tablespoon of the meat mixture in the center of the leaf. Fold in each side of the leaf. Beginning with the stem end and roll into a neat eggroll shaped package. Place seam side down in the prepared baking dish. Repeat the process until all of the meat mixture has been used. Drizzle the rolls with bacon drippings if desired. Gently pour tomato juice over the cabbage rolls to just cover. Bake for 1½ hours. Serve warm.

From the kitchen of Juanice Shoults

...'Love the Lord your God with all your heart and with all your soul and with all your mind.' This is the first and greatest commandment. And the second is like it: 'Love your neighbor as yourself.'
Matthew 22:37-39

Becky's Sour Cream Enchiladas

Serves 6-8

1 pound lean ground beef

½ cup chopped onion

½ teaspoon salt

8 corn tortillas

½ cup vegetable oil

½ cup taco sauce

1 cup shredded Monterrey Jack cheese, or more if desired

¼ cup butter

6 tablespoons flour

2 teaspoons chicken bullion

2 cups water

1 cup sour cream

½ cup chopped green chilies, fresh or canned

In a large frying pan, cook beef until browned. Drain unwanted drippings from the pan. Stir in onions and cook, stirring often, until onions are translucent. Stir in salt. Set aside.

Preheat oven to 400 degrees. Spray a 9" x 13" baking pan with non-stick spray. Set aside.

Add oil to a medium sized skillet and quickly fry tortillas one at a time until limp. Drain tortillas on paper towels.

Place one tortilla on work surface. Put a heaping tablespoon of meat mixture down center of tortilla. Top meat with 1 tablespoon taco sauce and sprinkling of cheese. Roll tortilla around meat and place seam side down in prepared baking pan. Repeat the procedure with all the tortillas. Set aside.

In a small saucepan, melt butter. Add flour and bullion. Stir until smooth. Mixing flour/butter mixture with a whisk, stir in water. Cook, stirring constantly, until thick. Remove from heat. Stir in sour cream and chilies. Pour over tortillas. Top with remaining cheese. Bake 15 to 20 minutes or until bubbly hot.

From the kitchen of Becky Shoults Bibb

"These appetizing Sour Cream Enchiladas of Becky's are always a popular, special treat!"
Tracy Shoults

"*We always love hearin' the old stories, 'bout how my dad used to play, as a kid in the old barn! We still love to take our kids out there, to let them 'treasure hunt' for some neat old relics!*"

Hunter Shoults

East Texas Casserole

Makes 8-10 servings

1 pound lean ground beef

1 green pepper, seeds removed and chopped

1 large yellow or white onion, chopped

3 stalks celery, sliced

1 large can of Ranch Style® beans

1 can diced tomatoes

1 can tomato sauce

1 teaspoon cumin

¾ cup uncooked Minute® rice

2 cups water

3 Tablespoons chili powder

½ pound Velveeta® cheese, cut into cubes, spicy or regular cheese to your taste

4 ounces tortilla chips, crushed

1 cup grated cheddar or monterrey jack cheese

¼ cup chopped green onion

In a large skillet, brown the beef. Remove the drippings from the pan if you desire. Stir in green pepper, onion, and celery. Cook, stirring often, until the veggies are tender. Add the beans, canned tomatoes, and tomato sauce. Stir well. Add the rice, water, chili powder, and cumin. Stir to blend ingredients and bring to a simmer. Cover the pan and cook on low heat for about two hours. Stir every 20 minutes. When mixture has thickened, stir in the Velveeta® cubes. Stir until the cheese has melted. Pour the mixture into a serving dish and top with grated cheese, crushed chips and chopped green onion.

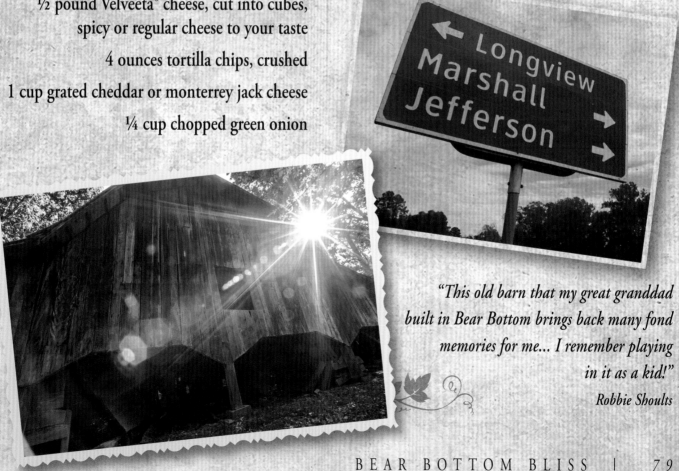

"This old barn that my great granddad built in Bear Bottom brings back many fond memories for me... I remember playing in it as a kid!"

Robbie Shoults

KING RANCH CHICKEN

Makes 12 servings

1 *(3 pound)* chicken or 4 chicken breasts, cooked and cut into bite-size pieces

1 can RoTel® tomatoes

1 can cream of mushroom soup

1 can cream of chicken soup

1 large onion, finely chopped

1 bell pepper, seeds removed and finely chopped

8 ounces pepper jack cheese, shredded

2 cups tortilla chips, crushed; or 8 corn tortillas, cut into quarters

Preheat oven to 350 degrees. Spray a 9" x 13" casserole dish with non-stick spray. Set aside.

In a large mixing bowl, combine chicken, RoTel® tomatoes, soups, onion, and bell pepper. Mix well. Set aside.

Put the tortilla chips or cut tortillas in the bottom of the prepared casserole dish. Evenly distribute the chicken mixture over the top of the tortillas. Bake for 30 minutes. Remove the casserole from the oven and top with shredded cheese. Return to the oven for 10 additional minutes. Serve warm.

From the kitchen of Anita Overhultz

SPAGHETTI SAUCE

Makes 8-10 servings

2 pounds lean ground meat

1 large white or yellow onion, finely chopped

1½ teaspoons salt

¼ cup Worcestershire® sauce

1 can tomato paste

1 can stewed tomatoes

1 can mushroom soup

Spaghetti cooked according to directions

In a large saucepan over medium-high heat, brown the meat. Remove any undesired pan drippings. Add the onion and stir well to blend. Continue cooking the mixture until the onions are translucent. Add the salt, Worcestershire®, tomato paste, and stewed tomatoes. Simmer the mixture over low heat for 45 minutes. Stir in the mushroom soup and continue to cook for 15 additional minutes. Serve warm over cooked pasta.

From the kitchen of Anita Overhultz

Corn & Bacon Casserole

Serves 12

1 Tablespoon olive oil

1 small yellow onion, finely chopped

2 cloves garlic, minced

4 green onion tops, chopped

1 *(14 ounce)* can whole kernel corn, drained

1 *(14 ounce)* can cream style corn

1 cup bacon bits or crumbled, cooked
Bear Creek Smokehouse bacon

2-4 jalapeño peppers, seeded and finely diced
(or 2-3 tablespoons diced pickled jalapeños)

4 ounces cream cheese, softened

4 Tablespoons butter, melted

1 cup shredded monterrey jack/
cheddar cheese blend *(divided)*

1 *(8 ounce)* package of corn muffin mix
we recommend Jiffy Corn Muffin Mix

Fresh sliced jalapeño peppers for garnish *(optional)*

Preheat oven to 350 degrees. Spray 9" x 13" casserole dish with non-stick spray. Set aside.

Heat olive oil in large non-stick skillet over medium heat. Sauté onion in olive oil until onion is translucent. Add garlic and cook one minute longer. Transfer onion mixture to small bowl. Set aside.

In a large bowl, combine corn, cream style corn, bacon bits, jalapeños, green onion tops, reserved onion mixture, softened cream cheese, melted butter, and ½ cup cheese. Mix well. Add cornbread mix from the package. Mix until blended. Pour into prepared casserole dish. Bake for 50 minutes or until top is golden. Sprinkle with remaining ½ cup cheese. Return to oven for 10 minutes. Serve warm. Garnish with fresh sliced peppers if desired.

- Bear Bottom Tall Tales By Bobby Shoults -

*"Back in the day, some of the ladies would bring their pans that they were going to cook in.
We'd always let them take their pan back to see which turkey would fit!
Sometimes it was hard to tell if it was them turkeys, or the ladies chasin' 'em around
creatin' all the ruckus!"*

"*The rugged beauty of the East Texas Piney Woods makes a perfect backdrop for the old abandoned barns of the area, and makes me glad I'm Texan!*"

Hunter Shoults

TERESA'S STUFF

Serves 4-6

1 pound hamburger meat

½ cup chopped onion

1 can cream of chicken soup

1 can cream of mushroom soup

1 box macaroni and cheese, prepared according to package directions

1 can RoTel® tomatoes

1 can whole kernel corn, drained

½ teaspoon garlic powder

Salt and pepper to taste
(optional to use ground cayenne pepper)

In a large skillet, brown meat and remove any unwanted fat. Add onion to the skillet. Cook over medium heat until onion is translucent. To the skillet, add soups, corn, RoTel, garlic powder, salt and pepper to taste. Stir in prepared macaroni and cheese. Continue cooking for about 15 minutes, stirring often. Serve warm.

From the kitchen of Teresa

- BEAR BOTTOM TALL TALES BY BOBBY SHOULTS -

"We built this smokehouse in 1972. It came about because of U.S.D.A. regulations and business growth... we had too much wood in the old buildin'. The tables and walls were all wood, makin' it near impossible to meet the new U.S.D.A. requirements. We weren't quite sure just what we were gonna do 'til the U.S.D.A. inspector pointed out that we could get a small business loan. So that's what we did!

When the smokehouse was finished in 1973, it had two brick ovens that could smoke 600 turkeys each, at one time! They had a hollowed-out space underneath which meant someone had to crawl beneath the building to light a fire for the ovens to burn that hickory firewood! Seems kinda' old-fashioned now, but it sure was cuttin' edge back in the day!"

TOMATO GRAVY

Serves 4-6

2 Tablespoons vegetable oil

1 medium onion, minced

1 clove garlic, minced

1 rib celery with leaves, finely chopped

2 cans tomato paste

1 *(6 ounce)* can tomato sauce

1½ cups water

3 tablespoons sugar

2 tablespoons salt

¼ teaspoon pepper

Prepared meatballs, if desired

Spaghetti cooked according to package directions

Parmesan cheese

Place oil in a large frying pan over medium heat. Sauté onion, garlic, and celery in the oil until tender.

Add tomato paste, sugar, salt and pepper. Bring to simmer for three minutes, stirring constantly.

Add tomato sauce and water. Bring to simmer for 45 minutes, stirring occasionally.

If using meatballs, add them at this point. Return pot to simmer for about one hour.

Serve sauce over prepared spaghetti. Sprinkle with Parmesan cheese if desired.

"The crude simplicity of the old cabins is a stark reminder of just how blessed we are today!"
Stacia Shoults

LASAGNA

Makes 12 servings

2 boxes lasagna noodles, cooked and drained according to package directions

3 Tablespoons olive oil

1 pound ground beef

1 onion, finely chopped

1 teaspoon garlic salt

8 ounces sour cream or ricotta

1 large can tomato sauce

½ cup water

16 ounces sliced or shredded mozzarella cheese

"Everything Anita makes is excellent and this Lasagna is no exception! We serve it with fresh, hot garlic bread!"
Erin Shoults Marino

Preheat oven to 325 degrees. Spray a 9" x 13" oven-safe casserole dish with non-stick spray. Set aside.

In a large skillet, heat olive oil over medium-high heat. Add ground meat and stir to break up the meat. Cook until the meat is brown. Add the chopped onion and garlic salt. Stir to blend and cook until the onion is translucent. Add tomato sauce and water. Stir to blend. Turn off the heat under the skillet. Place about a ½ cup of the meat mixture in the bottom of the prepared dish. Spread evenly over the bottom of the pan. Put a layer of lasagna noodles with sides of the noodles touching, lengthwise in the pan. Distribute one cup of the meat mixture evenly over the noodles. Place small dollops of sour cream or ricotta evenly over the meat. Top this layer with a layer of cheese. Continue building layers in this manner until the meat is all incorporated. Top the casserole with a layer of cheese. Bake for 30-40 minutes or until hot and bubbly.

From the kitchen of Anita Overhultz

DID YOU KNOW?

Hick Shoults' real name was Willard Hays Shoults. His two older brothers provided the nickname. It seems as a toddler he carried around an apron full of hard hickory nuts, asking any kind soul he could to help him crack his 'hicks'... so the nickname Hick stuck!

May the God of hope fill you with all joy and peace as you trust in him, so that you may overflow with hope...

Romans 15:13

Sweet Potato Casserole

Makes 12 servings

3 cups cooked sweet potatoes

2 cups brown sugar, divided

2 eggs

1 teaspoon vanilla

1 cup butter or margarine, melted, divided

2 Tablespoons orange zest

⅓ cup flour

1 cup chopped pecans

Preheat oven to 350 degrees. Spray a 9" x 13" casserole dish with non-stick spray. Set aside.

In a large mixing bowl, combine potatoes, one cup brown sugar, eggs, vanilla, ½ cup melted butter, and orange zest. Mix until the ingredients are well blended and fluffy. Pour into the prepared dish. Set aside.

In a small bowl, combine remaining one cup brown sugar, ½ cup melted butter, flour, and chopped pecans. Mix with a pastry blender or fork. Evenly distribute the nut mixture over the top of the sweet potatoes. Bake for 30 minutes or until the top of the potatoes is golden brown.

From the kitchen of Anita Overhultz

- Bear Bottom Ramblings By Robbie Shoults -

"I love to fish, and I owe that in part to my mom, Brenda. She always seemed ready to fish! There wasn't a prettier sight after a long day of school, than to pull up to the house and see mom standing by the car, poles loaded, ready to head to the 'Big Pond'!

We had many ponds on our property, but the 'Big Pond' was special, deep, spring-fed and full of fish! My great-granddaddy dug it with teams of mules and slips, a type of horse-drawn dirt moving implement. Seemed like every time we wet a hook, we caught a fish!

The only thing that could run us off was darkness after a beautiful Bear Bottom sunset! Doesn't seem quite as 'Big' now, but what a special place that was!"

BAKED BROCCOLI CHEESE RICE

Makes 12 servings

4 Tablespoons butter

4 cloves garlic, minced

¼ cup flour

2 cups milk

1 teaspoon Dijon mustard

½ teaspoon salt

¼ teaspoon freshly ground black pepper

2 ½ cups shredded cheddar/Monterrey Jack cheese blend, divided

⅓ cup shredded Parmesan cheese

3 cups cooked white or brown rice

2-3 cups cooked broccoli florets

3 Tablespoons minced jalapeño pepper

Preheat oven to 400 degrees. Spray a 9" x 13" casserole dish with non-stick spray. Set aside.

In a large saucepan, melt the butter. Add garlic and sauté briefly. Whisk in the flour and cook 3-4 minutes, stirring constantly. Add the milk and stir constantly until the mixture has thickened. Stir in the mustard. Add salt and pepper then taste for seasoning. Add more salt and pepper if desired. Add two cups of the cheese blend and the Parmesan. Stir until the cheese has melted. Remove from heat. Add the rice, broccoli, and jalapeños. Stir to coat the broccoli with the cheese sauce. Pour into the prepared casserole dish. Sprinkle the remaining ½ cup cheese over the top of the vegetables. Bake for 20-30 minutes or until bubbly and the cheese topping has melted. Allow to cool for 5 minutes before serving.

From the kitchen of Tracy Shoults

DID YOU KNOW?

Bear Bottom is located in a tiny, little portion of 'The Piney Woods,' which covers a 54,400-square-mile area of eastern Texas, northwestern Louisiana, southwestern Arkansas, and the southeastern corner of Oklahoma. The most dense forest lands lie in the eastern part of Texas in 'The Piney Woods' region. The 'Big Thicket' region of 'The Piney Woods,' just north of Houston, has the most dense woodlands. The 'Big Thicket' was mostly uninhabited until heavy settlement from the U.S. began in the mid-19th century, and was even used as a refuge by runaway slaves!

'Tater Skillet Supper

Makes 4-6 servings

2 slices Bear Creek Smokehouse®
bacon, cut into 1" pieces

1 package franks, cut into 1" pieces

½ cup chopped yellow or white onions

½ cup chopped bell pepper

1 can cream of chicken soup

4 ounces water

3 cups sliced cooked potatoes

1 can cut green beans, drained

Additional cooked crumbled
bacon for garnish if desired

In a large skillet, cook bacon, franks, onion, and bell pepper until vegetables are tender and bacon is lightly browned. Remove any unwanted drippings from the pan. Stir in soup, water, green beans, and potatoes. Continue cooking until all ingredients are thoroughly heated. Garnish with additional cooked bacon if desired. Serve warm.

"When the office is busy during the Holidays, we all pitch in and alternate bringing lunch! 'Tater Skillet Supper is always on the rotation and there's never anything left of it!"

Tracy Shoults

Did You Know?

Right after Hick and Nellie Shoults were married, Hick would ride his horse each day from their home in Lansing Switch, near Hallsville, out to the farm he worked in Bear Bottom.

"In 1936, my father bought the land, 580 acres, when it was cheap" Hick Shoults said. "He told me, 'Now if you'll go to work on it, I'll give you the land!"

That family farmland eventually grew to over 1,400 acres of East Texas piney woods, pastures and fields! Hick and Nellie, established one of Harrison County's most noteworthy businesses on that land near Bear Creek... the year was 1943 that the smokehouse began! That's the year Hick raised 640 turkeys for the markets and tables of the Marshall area!

Hick and Nellie Shoults' dream to have a business the whole family could share had come true... Bear Creek Smokehouse was in business!

BEAR BOTTOM BLISS *Meats*

CHICKEN CORDON BLEU

Makes 7 servings

7 skinless, boneless, chicken breast halves

7 slices Swiss cheese

7 slices ham, thinly sliced

4 Tablespoons flour

1½ teaspoons paprika

6 Tablespoons butter

Double all of the following amounts to provide enough gravy for mashed potatoes, if desired.

½ cup dry white wine

1 teaspoon chicken bouillon granules

1 Tablespoon cornstarch

1 cup heavy cream

Stacia Shoults

"This recipe is so easy-to-make and it always seems to add a special 'touch of class' to any occasion! Try making it using our Bear Creek Smokehouse ham for even more irresistible flavor... M'mmm sooooo good! Helpful Hint: Don't forget to take the toothpicks out! (Sorry, Hunter)!"

Stacia Shoults

One at a time, place chicken breasts between two pieces of waxed paper or plastic wrap. Pound each breast briefly to make the breast an even thickness. Working with one breast at a time, place a slice of ham and cheese over the breast. Remove any ham or cheese hanging over the edges of chicken. Kitchen scissors work best for this. Fold chicken in half and secure with a toothpick. Set aside.

In a flat pan or platter, mix the flour and paprika. Coat both sides of each breast in this mixture. When all breasts are prepared this way, heat the butter in a large skillet over medium-high heat. Cook the chicken in the butter, turning to lightly brown both sides. Remove chicken from the skillet when browned. Add the wine and bouillon granules to the skillet. Stir well to incorporate pan drippings with the wine. Reduce the heat to low. Place all chicken breasts in the skillet. Cover and simmer gently for 20-30 minutes or until the chicken is no longer pink and juices run clear. Remove the toothpicks and transfer the breasts to a warm platter. Set aside.

In a small bowl, blend the cornstarch into the cream. Whisk the cream mixture slowly into the skillet juices stirring constantly until thickened. Pour over the chicken. Serve immediately. The chicken can be served over rice or mashed potatoes.

From the kitchen of Stacia Shoults

SALISBURY STEAK

Makes 8 servings

1 *(14 ounce)* can condensed French onion soup

1 *(14 ounce)* can cream of mushroom soup

2 pounds lean ground beef

½ cup finely chopped onions

⅔ cup dry bread crumbs

1 egg

Add salt and pepper as desired

3 Tablespoons flour

⅔ cup ketchup

⅔ cup water

2½ Tablespoons Worcestershire® sauce

1 jar sliced mushrooms, drained

1¼ teaspoon dry mustard

Preheat oven to 375 degrees. Spray a 9" x 13" casserole dish with non-stick spray. Set aside.

In a large bowl, mix together ⅓ of both soups. Add beef, onions, bread crumbs, egg, and pepper. Mix well to evenly combine the ingredients. Shape the mixture into eight oval patties.

In a large skillet over medium-high heat, brown both sides of the patties. Put the browned patties into the prepared casserole dish. Set aside.

In a small bowl, blend flour with the remaining soups. Add ketchup, water, Worcestershire® sauce, mustard, and mushrooms. Pour this mixture over the browned patties. Cover the casserole dish, and bake for 40-45 minutes. Serve warm.

From the kitchen of Stacia Shoults

"Nothin' says home-cookin' like Salisbury Steak! Stacia says it's easy to make... I say it's easy to eat! A happy plate every single time!"
Hunter Shoults

BEEF TIPS

Serves 6-8

2 pounds beef stew meat or chuck roast cut into 1" cubes

2 Tablespoons vegetable oil

1 cup beef broth

2 Tablespoons soy sauce

⅓ cup red wine or cooking wine

1 clove garlic, minced

¼ teaspoon onion salt

1 pound fresh sliced mushrooms or one large can sliced mushrooms, drained *(optional)*

2 Tablespoons cornstarch

¼ cup water

Mix cornstarch in the water. Set aside.

In a large skillet on medium-high heat, brown meat in the vegetable oil. Add all ingredients except cornstarch mixture. Stir to blend ingredients. Bring to slow simmer and cover. Cook about one hour, stirring occasionally. Cook until the meat is fork-tender. Stir the cornstarch mixture to re-blend with the water and add to the meat, stirring constantly until the mixture thickens. Simmer for one minute. Serve over cooked rice.

The Battle Of San Jacinto -1895, Painting By Henry Arthur McArdle (1836 - 1908)

DID YOU KNOW?

A few days after the slaughter of Texians at the Alamo, on the command of Santa Anna, another important battle took place. This battle ultimately led to the formation of the Republic of Texas, it was fought near here, in East Texas! The Battle of San Jacinto, fought on April 21, 1836, in present-day Harris County, Texas, was the decisive battle of the Texas Revolution. Led by General Sam Houston, the Texian Army engaged and defeated General Antonio López de Santa Anna's Mexican army in a fight that lasted just 18 minutes!

Santa Anna, the President of Mexico, was captured and surrendered the following day and was held as a prisoner of war. Three weeks later, he signed the peace treaty that dictated that the Mexican army leave the region, paving the way for the Republic of Texas to become an independent country!

"Almost nothin' makes my heart soar quite like an East Texas 'Big Sky' on a cool, fall mornin'!"

Hunter Shoults

CHICKEN-FRIED STEAK & GRAVY

Variable servings

Cube steak or tenderized round
steak cut into serving portions

Salt and pepper

Flour

Canola oil

Milk

These are general directions. You'll need to adjust amounts of each ingredient according to the number of servings you are making.

In a pie plate, mix flour with salt and pepper. You can use seasoned salt or freshly ground or seasoned pepper. Stir with a fork to blend. Dredge meat portions in the flour to coat the entire surface of the meat. Set aside on waxed paper.

Cover the bottom of a large skillet with ¼" of canola oil. Place over medium-high heat. When the oil is heated, cook one or two steak portions at a time until browned on both sides and cooked through. Remove steaks to a plate or baking tray and set in a warm oven until all steaks are cooked. Add additional oil to the skillet during this process if necessary.

When all steaks are cooked, stir flour into the skillet. Stir constantly to mix the flour with the drippings. When the flour turns light brown, stir in milk. Lower the heat to medium. Stir constantly until the gravy thickens and is bubbly hot. Add more milk to adjust the consistency. Remove a small spoonful of the gravy so you can cool it and taste for seasoning. Add salt and pepper to your taste. Serve the gravy over the steaks.

Serve with mashed potatoes or french fries and warm homemade bread.

Do to others as you would have them do to you.

Luke 6:31

Marilyn's No-Fry Baked Chicken Breasts

Serves 4

2 eggs

1 sleeve round butter crackers,
we prefer Ritz® Crackers

½ teaspoon seasoned salt

4 boneless, skinless chicken breasts

"I love my Mar-Mar's chicken, it's soooo good!"
Cooper Shoults

Preheat oven to 350 degrees. Spray baking dish with non-stick spray. Set aside. Place the eggs in a medium bowl and beat well with a fork or whisk.

Pour the crackers into a zip top plastic bag. Add seasoned salt to the crackers and close the bag after removing excess air from the bag. Gently crush the crackers using a rolling pin or can. Empty the cracker crumbs into another medium bowl.

One at a time, dip each chicken breast first into beaten eggs, then into the cracker crumbs coating the entire chicken breast. Place the chicken breasts on the prepared baking dish. Bake 30-40 minutes or until juices run clear or until a meat thermometer indicates the chicken is thoroughly cooked.

From the kitchen of Marilyn Kennedy

Did You Know?

Back in the 40's, Bear Creek turkeys were personally delivered in a pickup truck under a bed of ice! Customers had to place their orders through the county agriculture extension office, since the Shoults' had no telephone! By the time they got a phone in 1949, they fast became good customers of 'Ma Bell'! By 1959, the family not only had a telephone, they had added an extension! The idea of a farm family with two phones on the property was so unheard of that the Shoults' second phone made news! That's when the telephone company took out an ad in all the farm magazines featuring the Shoults Family! The ad explained how much time was saved with the extension phone line from their home to the smokehouse... my how times have changed!

Stacia's Chicken Supreme

Serves 12

1 pound fresh broccoli, chop into bite size pieces, steam for 2 minutes

3 cups cooked chicken breasts, chopped into bite size pieces

⅓ cup butter, plus 1 stick butter for the cracker topping

¼ cup cornstarch

½ cup chicken broth

¼ teaspoon salt

¼ teaspoon pepper

2 cups milk

3 cups shredded cheddar cheese, divided

2 sleeves round butter crackers, we prefer Ritz® Crackers

1 Tablespoon poppy seeds

"This dish is so good! I love it when Stacia fixes it for our family!"
Krysta Shoults Coleman

Preheat oven to 350 degrees. Spray a 9" x 13" casserole dish with non-stick spray. Distribute the broccoli and chicken evenly in the pan. Set aside.

In a saucepan over medium heat, combine ⅓ cup butter, chicken broth, cornstarch, salt, pepper, and milk. Stir well to blend. Heat over medium heat, stirring often, until the sauce has thickened. Turn the heat to low and add 1½ cups of the cheddar cheese. Stir until the cheese has melted. Pour this mixture over the chicken and broccoli. Top with remaining cheese. Set aside.

Melt one cup of butter. Stir in the poppy seeds. Set aside.

Put the crackers in a large zip top bag. Slightly crush the crackers *(but not too small)*. Add the melted butter mixture to the crackers. Zip the bag shut and rotate the bag in your hands to distribute the butter evenly. Sprinkle the crumbs over the casserole. Bake for 30 minutes or until hot and bubbly.

From the kitchen of Stacia Shoults

No one can serve two masters. Either you will hate the one and love the other, or you will be devoted to the one and despise the other. You cannot serve both God and money.

Matthew 6:24

Parmesan Chicken

Makes 6 servings

6 boneless, skinless chicken breast halves

½ cup mayonnaise

½ cup plain Greek yogurt

½ cup grated fresh Parmesan cheese, plus additional ¼ cup for topping

1½ teaspoon seasoned salt

½ teaspoon ground black pepper

1 teaspoon garlic powder

Preheat oven to 375 degrees. Spray a 9" x 13" baking pan with non-stick spray. Place the chicken breasts in a single layer in the pan. Set aside.

In a small bowl, mix together the mayonnaise, yogurt, ½ cup of the cheese, salt, pepper, and garlic powder. Blend the ingredients together. Using a spatula, cover the chicken breasts with the mayonnaise mixture being careful to cover all exposed surfaces of the chicken. Sprinkle with remaining ¼ cup Parmesan cheese over the top of the chicken. Bake for 45 minutes. Serve warm or refrigerate covered and reheat the next day.

- Bear Bottom Ramblings By Robbie Shoults -

"I can remember one cold, crisp Bear Bottom morning my grandad took me deer hunting on our place! He had spotted a Buck at a distance, and motioned for me to be quiet and follow him to get in closer for a clean shot. I was trembling with excitement after seeing the Buck, as I followed my grandfather's every footstep, trying not to break a twig or crumple a leaf as we got in closer!

Just then, Pop raised the old 1800's saddle ring 30-30, that my great grandfather had traded cottonseed for, took aim and pulled the trigger! The blast sounded like an explosion that echoed through the woods forever!

I still have that set of antlers and the memories from my grandad's Bear Bottom Buck! I've also had a passion for hunting, from that day forward!"

Built in 1900, The Old Harrison County Courthouse
is located in the center of Whetstone Square in
Marshall, Texas and is one of the most famous
and admired buildings in Texas!

CHICKEN EXCELSIOR HOUSE

Makes 6 servings

6 chicken breast

Garlic salt

¼ pound butter

1 teaspoon paprika

3 Tablespoon lemon juice

1 carton sour cream

¼ cup sherry wine

1 can mushroom soup

A generous dash of cayenne pepper

Preheat oven to 375 degrees. Prepare baking pan by spraying with non-stick spray. Set aside.

Sprinkle the chicken with garlic salt. Melt the butter and add the paprika and lemon juice. Roll chicken in the butter mixture and place on the baking pan. Bake at 375 degrees for one hour or until tender. Mix sour cream, wine, and mushroom soup to make sauce. Pour over chicken and bake an additional 15 minutes.

From the kitchen of Nancy Shoults Palmer

DID YOU KNOW?

This flag was introduced to the Congress of the Republic of Texas on December 28, 1838, by Senator William H. Wharton and was adopted on January 25, 1839 as the final national flag of the Republic of Texas. When Texas became the 28th state of the Union on December 29, 1845, the national flag became the state flag. From 1879 until 1933 there was no official state flag, although the Lone Star remained the de facto state flag.
Texas was formally flagless until the passage of the Texas Flag Code in 1933.

GEMINI MOON PEBBLES *(BEAN BURGERS)*

Makes 4-6 servings

1 can chili

1 can Ranch Style® beans, undrained

¼ cup sweet pickle relish

¼ cup finely chopped onion

1 cup shredded cheddar cheese

4-6 packaged hamburger buns

"The kids love these Moon Pebbles! It's always my go-to recipe when I barely have enough time to throw dinner together!"

Tracy Shoults

Preheat broiler. Line a broiling pan with aluminum foil. Set aside.

In a mixing bowl, blend chili, beans, relish, onion, and cheese. Place bun bottoms cut-side facing up on one half of the baking pan. Place the bun tops with cut-side facing up on the other half of the baking pan. Spoon the chili mixture evenly over the bun bottoms. Place under the broiler until cheese is melted and chili mixture is heated throughout. It may be necessary to remove the bun tops during the cooking time to prevent them from burning. To serve, place the toasted bun tops on the bottoms with the chili mixture. Serve warm.

From the kitchen of Dorothy Newman

- BEAR BOTTOM TALL TALES BY BOBBY SHOULTS -

"We used to raise the turkeys... we don't any more!" My dad used to tell visitors...
"The only animal dumber than a turkey, is the man who raises 'em and tries to get by with it!"

"The coyotes would get 'em! They wouldn't eat 'em, they'd just kill 'em!

So 'bout a year or so after the smokehouse was completed, we quit raisin' the birds!
We started buyin' already dressed birds for the same price it had cost us to raise our own!
From then on it seemed like we started growin' fast and shippin' more each year!
I was jus' glad I didn't have to dress them birds out in the mud any more!
That was one of the best decisions we ever made!"

STUFFED PEPPERS

Makes 6 servings

6 bell peppers, any color of peppers you desire

Salt and pepper to taste

1 pound ground beef or turkey

⅓ cup chopped onion

2 cloves garlic, minced

1 *(14.5 ounce)* can whole peeled tomatoes, chopped

1 teaspoon Worcestershire® sauce

½ cup uncooked rice

½ cup water

1 cup shredded cheddar cheese

2 *(10.75 ounce)* cans condensed tomato soup

Water as needed

Bring a large pot of salted water to boil. Cut the tops off the peppers and remove the seeds. Cook peppers in simmering water for 3 minutes. Remove with tongs and drain. When peppers have cooled a little, sprinkle salt and pepper inside each one. Set aside.

In a large skillet, sauté the meat breaking it into small pieces as it cooks. Drain grease. Add the onions and cook an additional five minutes until the onions are translucent. Stir in the garlic during the final minute as the onions cook. Add the tomatoes, rice, ½ cup water, and Worcestershire® sauce. Cover, simmer for 15 minutes or until rice is tender. Remove from heat and stir in the cheese. Set aside.

Preheat the oven to 350 degrees. Spray a baking dish with non-stick spray. Set aside.

Stuff each pepper with the beef/turkey mixture and place *(open side up)* in the baking dish. Set aside.

In a medium bowl, combine soup with enough water to make a gravy consistency. Pour over and around the peppers. Cover the dish with a lid or foil. *(If using foil, create a tent with the foil to avoid contact with the peppers.)* Bake 25-35 minutes or until hot and bubbly. Serve warm.

Whoever does not love does not know God, because God is love.

1 John 4:8

PORK CHOP SUPREME

Makes 4 servings

4 lean pork chops, 1" thick

Salt and freshly ground black pepper

4 thin onion slices

4 thin lemon slices

¼ cup brown sugar, divided

¼ cup catsup, divided

"These are 'finger lickin' good!
Everyone A-L-W-A-Y-S comes back for more!"
Brenda Shoults

Preheat the oven to 350 degrees. Spray a 9" x 13" baking dish with non-stick spray. Set aside.

Season both sides of all pork chops with salt and pepper. Place the pork chops in the prepared baking dish. Top each pork chop with an onion slice then a lemon slice. Spoon one Tablespoon of catsup on top of each pork chop assembly, then sprinkle one Tablespoon of brown sugar on each. Cover the pan with foil and bake for 1 hour. Remove the foil and baste each pork chop with pan drippings. Return to the oven and bake for an additional 15-20 minutes. Serve warm.

Our Favorite Meat Loaf

Makes 8-10 servings

8 ounces tomato sauce

¼ cup brown sugar

¼ cup white vinegar

1 teaspoon prepared mustard

1 egg

1 onion, minced

¼ cup saltine cracker crumbs

2 pounds lean ground beef

1½ teaspoons salt

¼ teaspoon pepper

Preheat oven to 350 degrees.

In a small bowl, combine tomato sauce, brown sugar, vinegar, and mustard. Set aside.

In a large bowl, mix the meat, egg, onions, cracker crumbs, salt and pepper. Add ½ of the tomato sauce mixture. Mix well. Shape the meat into an oval loaf and place in an oblong baking pan. Make a depression in the top of the loaf and pour the remaining tomato sauce into the depression. Bake for 25-30 minutes or until center of the loaf tests done with a meat thermometer. Remove from oven and let stand for 10 minutes before cutting to serve.

SWEET & SPICY BACON CHICKEN

Makes 4 servings

4 chicken breasts, cut lengthwise into thirds

12 slices Bear Creek Smokehouse® bacon

Salt and pepper

Garlic powder

Chili powder, if desired

⅔ cup brown sugar

"This recipe combines the irresistible flavor of bacon with sweet brown sugar! For a special twist, try cooking them on the grill!"
Erin Shoults Marino

Preheat oven to 400 degrees. Spray a casserole dish with non-stick spray. Set aside.

Season the chicken pieces by sprinkling with salt, pepper, garlic powder, and chili powder. Wrap each piece of chicken with a strip of bacon. Secure bacon with a toothpick, if desired. Put the brown sugar on a plate and roll each chicken piece in the brown sugar. Place the chicken pieces in a single layer in the prepared dish. Bake 30-40 minutes or until the chicken is cooked through and the bacon is brown and crispy. *(The prepared chicken pieces can also be cooked on a pre-heated grill).*

From the kitchen of Tracy Shoults

DID YOU KNOW?

The American Black Bear once roamed throughout the state of Texas!

Black Bears were almost gone in Texas by the end of WW II, due to unregulated hunting and habitat loss.

For nearly a century, the Bears were hunted for their meat, fat for cooking, and hides for tanning, as well as, for the sport of competitive hunting, even attracting top bear enthusiast, Teddy Roosevelt! Over the years, Bear numbers dwindled until only a few regions held established Bear populations.

Now, due to diligent conservation efforts, Black Bears are again steadily returning to their natural habitat in the swamps and thickets of the Big Thicket Region of East Texas!

The Texas Parks and Wildlife Department has documented several reliable bear sightings in recent years throughout East Texas! Studies are also being conducted by researchers at Stephen F. Austin State University, to better determine the distribution and population of Black Bears in East Texas.

Tracy & Robbie Shoults

BAKED MUSHROOM MEAT LOAF

Serves 4

1 *(3 ounce)* can sliced mushrooms, drain liquid into measuring cup and reserve

Milk

2 eggs

½ cup chili sauce

1 teaspoon Worcestershire sauce

2 teaspoons salt

½ teaspoon dried thyme

1 cup dried bread crumbs

1½ pounds ground chuck

½ pound ground pork

2 head-boiled eggs, peeled and each egg cut into 8 wedges

1 Tablespoon grated parmesan cheese

1 Tablespoon chopped parsley

Preheat oven to 350 degrees. Spray 11" x 7" x 1½" baking dish with non-stick spray. Set aside.

Add enough milk to reserved mushroom liquid to equal one cup. In a large bowl, beat eggs slightly. Stir in milk/mushroom liquid mixture, chili sauce, Worcestershire, salt, thyme, and bread crumbs. Mix lightly with fork until bread crumbs are moistened. Add raw meats. Mix ingredients until well combined, using clean hands if necessary to mix. Spoon ½ of the meat mixture into the center of the prepared baking dish and form into a 9" x 5" rectangle. Arrange egg wedges and mushroom slices over the mixture. Sprinkle with cheese and parsley. Top with remaining meat mixture. Carefully shape into a loaf shape. Bake one hour and 15 minutes or until meat is cooked throughout.

CHICKEN ENCHILURRITOS

Makes 12 servings

Pink dip *(see page 23 for recipe)*

3 boneless chicken breasts

Tortillas

Olive oil

Taco seasoning

1/2 red onion diced

2 cloves of garlic minced

Dollop of sour cream

1 cup each of shredded cheddar and jack cheese

Cayenne Pepper, if desired

Optional Garnishes:
Cilantro, diced tomatoes, sour cream, and scallions

"Hunter craves Tex-Mex all day, every day! This is such a fun, new take on traditional Chicken Enchiladas! We make this all the time and there are never any leftovers!"
Stacia Shoults

Season the chicken with salt and pepper. Heat olive oil in a pan and begin cooking the chicken. Sprinkle chicken with taco seasoning *(and cayenne pepper if desired)* before flipping. Cook on both sides until the juices run clear and the chicken is no longer pink. Remove chicken and place on a plate to cool. Add onion and garlic to the pan and saute in the grease. Once the onions become translucent, stir in the Pink Dip and let heat on low heat. Stir in the Sour Cream.

Shred chicken with two forks.

Meanwhile, warm tortillas in a skillet or in the microwave. If you prefer to use the microwave, pile four tortillas up and place them under a damp paper towel. Microwave 30 seconds at a time until they are warm.

Place a large spoonful of the Pink Dip in one tortilla followed by placing desired amount of shredded chicken in the tortilla and roll. Once rolled, place seam side down in a baking dish. Repeat step until all chicken is gone. Spread the rest of the pink dip over the stops of the rolled tortillas. Sprinkle with shredded Cheddar and Jack cheese. Bake for 10-15 Minutes at 350 degrees until the cheese has melted. Remove from oven and serve warm. Garnish as desired, serve with beans and rice.

From the kitchen of Stacia Shoults

Chicken Tetrazzini

Makes 12 servings

1½ - 2 cups diced, cooked chicken

2 cups chicken stock

1½ cups cooked noodles, drained

1½ cups diced celery

1 *(4 ounce)* can sliced mushrooms, drained

1 tomato, peeled, seeds removed and chopped

1 Tablespoon minced green bell pepper

⅓ cup chopped onion

1 clove garlic, minced

½ pound *(or more)* shredded cheese

1 Tablespoon chopped parsley

2 Tablespoons white wine

Salt and pepper to taste

½ cup dry bread crumbs

4 Tablespoons cold butter, cut into thin slices

"This tasty Chicken Tetrazzini recipe has been in our family for years! It's always a favorite when I make it for our family!"
Brenda Shoults

Preheat oven to 350 degrees. Spray a 13" x 9" casserole dish with non-stick spray. Set aside.

In a large saucepan, combine the chicken stock, wine, celery, tomato, bell pepper, onion, and garlic. Bring to a simmer and cook for 5 minutes or until onions are translucent. Stir in the chicken, noodles, parsley, and mushrooms. Taste for seasoning and add salt and pepper to your taste. Pour the mixture into the prepared casserole dish. Sprinkle cheese over the top. Evenly distribute the bread crumbs over the dish. Dot the butter slices evenly over the surface of the casserole. Bake 25-30 minutes or until hot and bubbly. Serve warm.

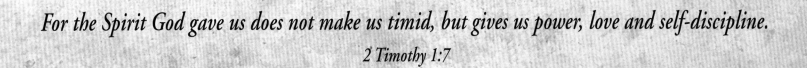

For the Spirit God gave us does not make us timid, but gives us power, love and self-discipline.
2 Timothy 1:7

PORK CARNITAS

Makes 8-10 servings

4 pound boneless pork butt, fat removed and cut into 2" cubes

1½ teaspoons salt

¾ teaspoon pepper

1 teaspoon ground cumin

1 onion, cleaned and cut into quarters

2 bay leaves

1 teaspoon dried oregano

2 Tablespoons fresh lime juice

1½ cups water

1 orange, juiced, also use the spent halves

Combine all ingredients in a slow cooker. Cook for eight hours on low heat setting. Meanwhile, line a baking pan with foil. After eight hours, use a large slotted spoon to remove the meat from the slow cooker and place on the prepared baking pan. Discard the orange halves and bay leaves. Set the meat aside to cool.

Pour the liquids from the slow cooker into a saucepan. Put the saucepan over a burner with medium-high heat and bring to a boil. Cook until the sauce has reduced to about one cup of liquid. While the sauce is reducing, break apart or shred the pork using two forks. When the sauce has reduced, add the shredded pork. Taste for seasoning and add salt and/or pepper if desired. Spread the meat mixture evenly over the foil lined pan. Place the pan in the center of the oven and set the oven to broil. Remove from the broiler when the top and edges of the meat are well-browned and slightly crispy. This will take 5-8 minutes. Using a wide spatula, flip the meat to expose the bottom of the meat and continue broiling until the top is slightly crispy. Serve immediately with tortillas and toppings.

From the kitchen of Laverna Browning

God is our refuge and strength, an ever-present help in trouble.

Psalm 46:1

BEAR BOTTOM BLISS *Veggies*

CHEESY MASHED POTATOES

Serves 4-6

2 pounds potatoes

½ teaspoon garlic powder

¼ cup shredded cheddar cheese, plus 1 cup shredded cheddar cheese for topping

¼ cup milk

½ cup sour cream

6 ounces cream cheese, softened

Salt and pepper to taste

Peel potatoes and put in large saucepan or pot and cover with water. Bring to simmer. Cook potatoes until they are fork tender. Drain.

Preheat oven to 375 degrees. Spray baking dish with non-stick spray. Set aside.

Place potatoes in large bowl and mash. Add all ingredients except one cup cheese, salt and pepper. Mix well. Taste for seasoning and add salt and pepper to your taste. Place potatoes in prepared baking dish. Top with remaining cheddar cheese. Bake until cheese has melted.

From the kitchen of Stacia Shoults

ENGLISH PEAS & PEPPERED BACON

Makes 6-8 servings

2 cups frozen English peas

2 shallots, diced

4-5 slices Bear Creek Smokehouse® peppered bacon

2 teaspoons sugar

1 stick butter

Salt and freshly ground black pepper to taste *(be generous with the pepper)*

In a large skillet, sauté the bacon until crisp. Remove the bacon to drain on folded paper towels. Crumble the bacon when cooled. Set aside.

Remove all but a few teaspoons of the bacon drippings from the skillet. Sauté the shallots until they soften. To the shallots, add the butter, sugar, and crumbled bacon. Stir in the peas. Season the mixture to taste with salt and pepper. Simmer gently until the peas are thoroughly heated. Serve warm.

From the kitchen of Tracy Shoults

Green Rice Dressing

Serves 4

2 cups white rice, we prefer Minute Rice®

2¾ cups water, boiling

½ teaspoon salt

2 eggs

⅔ cup vegetable oil

1 small can evaporated milk, we prefer Pet® milk

2 cups shredded sharp cheddar cheese

½ cup grated onion

1 small can sliced or chopped mushrooms

Salt and pepper, to taste

1 cup chopped parsley leaves

2 cans mushroom soup

Combine rice and boiling water in large glass or metal mixing bowl. Let stand for 15 minutes.

Preheat oven to 350 degrees. Spray casserole dish with non-stick spray. Set aside.

In a small bowl, beat eggs. Add oil and milk, blending well with whisk. Stir in soup. Set aside.

Add remaining ingredients to the rice and stir well. Stir in egg mixture. Pour into prepared casserole dish. Bake for about one hour or until slightly browned on top and mixture is set.

From the kitchen of Mrs. Sasser

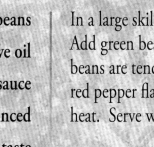

Samantha McDonald

Spicy Sautéed Green Beans

Makes 8-10 servings

1 bag frozen green beans

2 teaspoons olive oil

2 Tablespoons soy sauce

3-4 cloves garlic, minced

Crushed red pepper flakes, to taste

In a large skillet, heat olive oil over medium heat. Add green beans and cook, stirring often until the beans are tender. Add the garlic, soy sauce, and red pepper flakes. Cook for 5-10 minutes over low heat. Serve warm.

From the kitchen of Samantha McDonald

"A delightful, zesty dish from my daughter, Samantha!"
Tracy Shoults

Jalapeño Rice

Makes 4-6 servings

2 cups long grain rice

¼ cup vegetable oil

2 cups chopped onion

3-4 jalapeño peppers, seeds removed and finely diced

4 beef bouillon cubes

4 cups water

1 pound Velveeta cheese, cut into 1" cubes

1 stick butter

In a large skillet over medium-high heat, sauté rice in oil, stirring constantly until rice turns translucent. Add onions and jalapeños. Cook, stirring constantly about five minutes, or until onions are translucent and slightly brown. Add remaining ingredients. Stir well and bring to simmer. Cover, turn heat to lowest setting, and cook for 30-40 minutes, stirring every 10 minutes. Adjust cooking time if necessary cooking until water has been absorbed into rice. Serve warm.

From the kitchen of Muriel LaGrone

Decorated Corn

Makes 4-6 servings

2 Tablespoons butter, melted

8 ounces cream cheese, softened

2 cans whole kernel corn, drained

4 ounce can chopped green chilies

¼ cup milk

¼ teaspoon salt

½ teaspoon garlic salt

Pepper to taste

Preheat oven to 350 degrees. Spray a 9" x 9" baking dish with non-stick spray. Set aside.

In a large bowl, mix cream cheese and milk until well blended. Add butter and stir to combine. Add remaining ingredients and stir until well blended. Pour into prepared baking dish. Bake for 25-30 minutes or until well heated throughout.

...Do not be afraid; do not be discouraged.
Be strong and courageous....

Joshua 10:25

String Bean & English Pea Casserole

Serves 4

1 *(14.5 ounce)* can green beans, drained

1 *(14.5 ounce)* can English peas, drained

2 Tablespoons bacon drippings

½ medium onion, finely chopped

2 cups shredded cheddar cheese

1 can cream of mushroom soup

Salt and pepper to taste

1 cup dried bread crumbs

"This String Bean & English Pea Casserole is perfect for family suppers or even potluck dinner at church!"
Tracy Shoults

Preheat oven to 350 degrees. Spray a 9" x 9" baking pan with non-stick spray.

Place green beans in bottom of prepared baking pan. Drizzle bacon drippings evenly over green beans. Top the beans with ½ of the chopped onions and one cup of the cheese. Distribute English peas over the top of the green bean mixture. Sprinkle with remaining onions and cheese. Add salt and pepper to taste.

Pour mushroom soup evenly over the top of beans/pea mixture. Top with bread crumbs. Bake for about 20 minutes or until bubbly hot. Serve warm.

Scalloped Potatoes

Makes 6-8 servings

1 can cream of mushroom soup

½ cup milk

½ teaspoon salt

¼ teaspoon freshly ground black pepper

4 cups thinly sliced potatoes

1 onion, finely chopped

1 cup grated cheddar cheese

3 Tablespoons butter, divided

Dash of paprika

Preheat oven to 375 degrees. Use one Tablespoon of butter to grease a 1½ quart casserole dish. Set aside.

In a small mixing bowl, combine the soup, milk, salt, and pepper. Alternate layers of potatoes, onions, and sauce in the prepared dish. Top with grated cheese. Cut the remaining butter into thin slices and place them over the top of the cheese. Sprinkle with paprika. Cover the dish with aluminum foil and bake for one hour. Remove the foil and bake 15 additional minutes. Serve warm.

*"I'm always awestruck by Eagle's Nest at Caddo Lake!
It's a strange world that seems to disappear behind walls
of impenetrable Cypress groves, broken only by narrow,
twisting ribbons of open water passageways!"*

Robbie Shoults

STIR-FRIED CABBAGE

Serves 4

1 head of cabbage, shredded

12 ounces Bear Creek Smokehouse® Bacon, cooked, drained, and crumbled

1 package Bear Creek Smokehouse® Polish Sausage, cut into 1" pieces

1 onion, chopped

2 Tablespoons butter

Salt and pepper to taste

Add all ingredients to large skillet, wok, or Dutch oven over medium-high heat. Stir often until cabbage is no longer crisp. Serve warm.

From the kitchen of Reba Coxen

"An appetizing, change-of-pace recipe, made even more special using smoked Polish Sausage!"
Tracy Shoults

...those who hope in the Lord will renew their strength. They will soar on wings like eagles; they will run and not grow weary, they will walk and not be faint.

Isaiah 40:31

POTATO CASSEROLE

Makes 6-8 servings

32 ounces frozen hash brown potatoes, chopped

1 cup butter, melted, divided

1 can cream of chicken soup

12 ounces shredded cheddar cheese

8 ounces sour cream

1 teaspoon salt

½ onion, minced

1 cup Corn Flakes® cereal, crushed

"Anything with potatoes and cheese is sure to please me! Tracy definitely knows her way around the kitchen because when she makes this, I come running!"
Stacia Shoults

Preheat oven to 350 degrees. Spray a 9" x 13" casserole dish with non-stick spray. Set aside.

In a bowl, mix ½ cup melted butter, chicken soup, sour cream, and salt. Set aside.

Put the potatoes in an even layer in the prepared dish. Evenly distribute the onion and cheese over the potatoes. Pour the soup mixture over the top of the vegetables. Spread the mixture to cover the entire surface of the potatoes. Sprinkle the crushed cereal evenly over the surface and drizzle the remaining butter evenly over the cereal. Bake 45-50 minutes or until the top is lightly browned and the potatoes are bubbly.

From the kitchen of Tracy Shoults

SPICY PURPLE HULL PEAS

Makes 4-6 servings

2 pounds fresh or frozen purple hull peas

6 cups water

½ medium yellow onion, chopped

1 *(10 ounce)* can diced tomatoes with green chilies

7 ounces smoked sausage, sliced in 1" pieces

¼ teaspoon black pepper

Salt to taste

In a Dutch oven, put peas and fill with enough water to cover peas. Bring to a rolling boil and cook for 15 minutes.

Add onion, tomatoes, green chilies, salt and pepper.

Return to boil. Reduce heat to maintain a slow simmer. Cook for 10 to 15 minutes. Stir in sausage pieces. Serve warm.

From the kitchen of Minnie Wise

CORN CASSEROLE

Makes 4-6 servings

1 box corn muffin mix, we prefer Jiffy® Corn Muffin Mix

8 ounces sour cream

16 ounces cream style corn

2 eggs

1 stick butter or margarine

2-3 diced jalapeńos

1 cup shredded cheese

Preheat oven to 325 degrees.

Put the butter in a 9" x 9" glass baking dish and microwave just until the butter has melted. Stir in the corn, sour cream, jalapeńos, and cheese. Add the eggs and stir to blend thoroughly. Add the cornbread mix and stir well. Bake for 45 minutes or until the top is golden brown.

From the kitchen of Tracy Shoults

...enjoy choice food and sweet drinks, and send some to those who have nothing prepared. This day is holy to our Lord....

Nehemiah 8:10

"As a kid, I remember climbing up on the old Texas & Pacific
Steam Engine, originally built in 1915! It's now on permanent
display at the T&P Railway Museum in Marshall, Texas!"
Robbie Shoults

MERRY SQUASH BAKE

Makes 4-6 servings

4 squash cut into ¼" slices

1 onion, chopped

1 bell pepper, seeds removed and chopped

1 egg

1 can cream of chicken soup

1-2 cloves garlic, minced

½ stick butter or margarine, melted

1 cup of crushed Waverly Club® crackers

1 cup shredded cheddar or Jack cheese

Preheat oven to 350 degrees. Spray a casserole dish with non-stick spray. Set aside.

In a small bowl, combine the egg, soup, garlic, and melted butter. Set aside.

In a large bowl, combine the squash, onion, and bell pepper. Add the crushed crackers and shredded cheese. Toss lightly to evenly mix. Pour the soup mixture over vegetable mixture and toss lightly to combine. Place vegetable mixture in the prepared casserole dish. Cover dish with aluminum foil and bake for 30-40 minutes. Serve warm.

From the kitchen of Merry LaGrone Bagley

SQUASH DRESSING

Makes 4-6 servings

1 onion, chopped finely

1 stick butter or margarine

2 cups squash, sliced or chopped

2 eggs

1 can cream of mushroom soup

2 cups crumbled cooked cornbread

Preheat oven to 350 degrees. Spray a casserole dish with non-stick spray. Set aside.

In a large skillet, melt butter. Add onion and sauté until onion is translucent. Stir in squash and mix well. Set aside off the heat.

In a large bowl, mix the soup and eggs together. Add the crumbled cornbread and vegetables. Fold the ingredients together gently. Pour into the prepared baking dish. Bake for one hour or until the top and edges are golden brown. Serve warm.

AU GRATIN POTATOES WITH SMOKED HAM

Makes 6-8 servings

4 large Russet potatoes cut into thin slices

1½ cups heavy cream

½ cup milk

2 Tablespoons flour

3-4 cloves garlic, minced

1 teaspoon salt

Freshly ground pepper to taste

1 cup shredded cheddar cheese

1 cup diced Bear Creek Smokehouse® ham

Preheat oven to 400 degrees. Spray a casserole dish with non-stick spray. Set aside.

In a mixing bowl, whisk together the cream, milk, flour, garlic, salt and pepper. Set aside.

Place ⅓ of the potato slices in the bottom of the prepared dish. Add ½ of the ham. Pour ⅓ of the cream mixture over the potatoes. Repeat the layers ending with the remaining cream mixture. Cover the dish with foil and bake for 30 minutes. Remove the foil and bake 20 minutes longer. Add the shredded cheese to the top of the potatoes and bake an additional 5 minutes or until the cheese has melted. Serve warm.

From the kitchen of Tracy Shoults

Tracy Shoults

"The cheesy goodness of this recipe always makes it a guaranteed hit in our house!"

Erin Shoults Marino

BAKED SQUASH

Makes 6-8 servings

4 Tablespoons butter

4 Tablespoons olive oil

1 onion, finely chopped

4 cups sliced or roughly chopped squash

8 ounces sour cream

1 cup bread crumbs

"This buttery Baked Squash dish is always a welcome addition to any of our family gatherings!"
Brenda Shoults

Preheat oven to 350 degrees. Spray a casserole dish with non-stick spray. Set aside.

In a large skillet, heat the butter and olive oil over medium heat. Add the onions and sauté until the onions are translucent. Add the squash to the skillet and stir well. Cover the skillet and cook for 10 minutes or until the squash is tender. Use a potato masher to partially mash the squash. Stir in the sour cream. Pour vegetables into the prepared casserole dish. Sprinkle bread crumbs evenly over the top of the vegetables. Bake for 15-20 minutes or until the crust is golden brown. Serve warm.

CREAMY SQUASH

Makes 8-10 servings

1½ pounds yellow squash, cut into ¼" slices

1 can cream of chicken soup

8 ounces sour cream

1 jar pimento, drained and chopped

1 can sliced water chestnuts, drained

2 medium onions, finely chopped

1 stick butter or margarine

8 ounces stuffing mix

Preheat oven to 350 degrees. Spray a casserole dish with non-stick spray. Set aside.

Put the squash slices in a large saucepan and cover with water. Bring to a boil then drain. To the squash, add onions, butter, soup, sour cream, pimento, and water chestnuts. Mix gently to blend. Fold in the stuffing mix, taking care to keep the mixture fluffy. Pour the squash mixture into the prepared casserole dish. Bake for 30-40 minutes or until hot and bubbly.

From the kitchen of Melba Pollard

SCALLOPED POTATOES & HAM

Makes 6-8 servings

1 can cream of celery soup

½ cup milk

1½ cups diced Bear Creek Smokehouse® ham

½ cup thinly sliced onion

½ cup shredded cheddar cheese

3 cups thinly sliced potatoes

½ teaspoon black pepper

½ teaspoon paprika

Preheat oven to 375 degrees. Spray 1½ quart casserole dish with non-stick spray. Set aside.

In a bowl, combine soup, milk, and pepper. Set aside.

In the prepared casserole dish, alternate layers of potatoes, ham, onion, and soup mixture. Cover the dish with aluminum foil and bake for one hour. Remove from oven. Remove foil and distribute the cheese over the potato mixture. Sprinkle with paprika. Return the dish to the oven and bake 15 minutes. Serve warm.

DID YOU KNOW?

Back in the early days, the Shoults family ran a full-fledged farming and ranching operation!

Numerous feed salesmen, county extension agents as well as fertilizer and equipment reps who frequently visited Hick Shoults at the farm, would often visit right around lunch time... for good reason!

You see, Nellie Shoults, known as 'MeMaw' around Bear Bottom, was known far and wide as an amazingly good cook!

So daily, she would go through the routine of preparing a big home-cooked meal, fit for a king, and always enough to feed an army! Lunch always featured an abundance of farm fresh ingredients, grown right here in Bear Bottom soil!

So, Hick and Nellie, being the hospitable folks they were, always invited any guest who 'happened' by to enjoy a delicious home-cooked meal! Needless to say, there was never a shortage of guests, or great food!

In fact, some of the selected recipes in this Cookbook are from Nellie's collection of treasured recipes!

SUPER GARLIC & ROSEMARY NEW POTATOES

Makes 6-8 servings

2 pounds small red potatoes

½ cup extra virgin olive oil

1 teaspoon kosher salt

3 Tablespoons minced garlic

3 Tablespoons minced fresh rosemary leaves

"I still have this recipe, handwritten by Erin, from 1999. It's just as good today as it was then!"
Robbie Shoults

Preheat oven to 400 degrees. Spray a baking sheet with non-stick spray. Set aside.

Combine olive oil and garlic in a large Ziploc bag. Set aside.

Clean the potatoes and dry on paper towels. Slice each potato into quarters. Add sliced potatoes to the zip bag and close. Shake well to evenly coat the potato pieces with the seasoned oil.

Spread the potatoes over the prepared baking sheet. Sprinkle with the salt and minced rosemary. Bake for 45-60 minutes or until the potatoes are lightly browned and cooked throughout.

From the kitchen of Erin Shoults Marino

Erin Shoults Marino

Brenda's Squash Casserole

Makes 4-6 servings

3 Tablespoons olive oil

4 cups sliced squash, cut in ¼" thick slices

1 large onion, cut in ¼" slices
and separated into rings

2 cloves garlic, finely minced

1 bell pepper, seeds discarded and
finely chopped (optional)

1 can cream of mushroom soup

1 can mushroom stems and pieces, drained

½ cup sour cream

3 Tablespoons seasoned bread crumbs

½ cup grated cheddar cheese

Preheat oven to 350 degrees. Spray a casserole dish with non-stick spray. Set aside.

Put olive oil in a large skillet over medium-high heat. Add squash, onion, and bell pepper *(if desired)*. Sauté until onions are translucent. Add the garlic. Stir to blend. Add soup, mushrooms, sour cream. Stir well. Pour into the prepared dish. Sprinkle with bread crumbs and top with cheese. Bake 20-25 minutes or until cheese is melted and vegetables are bubbly hot. Serve warm.

From the kitchen of Brenda Shoults

"Thanks to Bobby's love of gardening, I always have plenty of squash on hand to make this casserole with homegrown squash!
Brenda Shoults

LAREDO RANCH BEANS

Makes 8-10 servings

1 pound dried pinto beans

8 cups water

½ pound Bear Creek Smokehouse® salt pork, diced into ½" cubes

1 clove garlic, minced

2 cups chopped onion

2 Tablespoons Worcestershire® sauce

1 teaspoon chili powder

1 teaspoon prepared mustard

2 cups canned crushed tomatoes

½ teaspoon salt

¼ teaspoon black pepper

Carefully wash and sort the beans removing any debris. Place the washed beans in a large kettle or Dutch oven. Add the water and salt pork. Bring to a boil, reduce the heat and simmer for one hour. Add the remaining ingredients. Cover the kettle and cook over low heat for 30 minutes. Remove the cover and continue to cook over low heat for an additional 30 minutes. Serve warm.

From the kitchen of Minnie Wise

"These Laredo Ranch Beans are irresistible! Great served with cornbread!"

Brenda Shoults

...go out in joy and be led forth in peace; the mountains and hills will burst into song before you, and all the trees of the field will clap their hands.

Isaiah 55:12

POTATO CASSEROLE

Makes 6-8 servings

32 ounces frozen hash brown potatoes, chopped

1 cup butter, melted, divided

1 can cream of chicken soup

12 ounces of shredded cheddar cheese

8 ounces of sour cream

1 teaspoon salt

½ onion, minced

1 cup Corn Flakes® cereal, crushed

Preheat oven to 350 degrees. Spray a 9" x 13" casserole dish with non-stick spray. Set aside.

In a bowl, mix ½ cup melted butter, chicken soup, sour cream, and salt. Set aside.

Put potatoes in an even layer in the prepared dish. Evenly distribute onion and cheese over potatoes. Pour soup mixture over the top of the vegetables. Spread the mixture to cover the entire surface of the potatoes. Sprinkle the crushed cereal evenly over the surface and drizzle the remaining butter evenly over the cereal. Bake 45-50 minutes or until the top is lightly browned and the potatoes are bubbly.

- BEAR BOTTOM RAMBLINGS BY ROBBIE SHOULTS -

"I can remember as a kid, following Pop around while he worked from sun up 'til sun down!

One hot summer day, I followed him to Caney Creek to help with the irrigation pump that pulled water from the creek, to irrigate the fields of Coastal Bermuda we used for hay!

I was only about five years old and probably not much help but I enjoyed being with Pop! He was tinkering with that old pump while I was on the creek bank in the shade!

Suddenly, he gives the rope a swift jerk to fire up the pump knocking me, boots and all right into the creek where I promptly sunk like a rock! Knowing I couldn't swim, he jumped in after me, clothes and all, to pull me out by the collar!

That cold creek sure felt good that hot east Texas day... and boy did we have a tale to tell!"

Zippy Zucchini Skillet

Serves 4

2 Tablespoons vegetable oil

4 medium zucchini or yellow squash, thinly sliced

1 medium yellow onion, chopped

1 *(16 ounce)* can whole kernel corn, drained

1 *(4 ounce)* can chopped green chilies

2 teaspoons jalapeño peppers, chopped with seeds removed, optional

¼ teaspoon salt

⅛ teaspoon garlic powder

½ cup shredded cheddar cheese

Heat oil in large skillet. Sauté squash and onion about 10 minutes or until tender. Stir in remaining ingredients *(except cheese)*. Cook while stirring occasionally until thoroughly heated. Remove from heat and stir in cheese. Serve warm.

From the kitchen of Minnie Wise

"This zesty recipe of Minnie's always hits the spot!"

Hunter Shoults

DID YOU KNOW?

In 1841, a new seat was sought for Harrison County and a local settler named Peter Whetstone offered up some of his land in central Harrison County on which to build the new city!

County commissioners were initially concerned that the water in the area would not be good... as this had been the major reason for moving the county seat from sites on the Sabine River, along with poor water quality, they had also been prone to disease and flooding!

However, Whetstone allegedly convinced the commissioners that the water was indeed good by pulling a jug of whiskey out of a hollow oak tree in what is now downtown Marshall!

He passed around the jug in hopes that he could get commissioners drunk enough to change their minds!

Whetstone's friend, Isaac Van Zandt, laid out the city and named it in honor of John Marshall.

The city was formally incorporated in 1841 by the Republic of Texas.

MEXICAN STREET CORN

Makes 6 servings

1 *(16 ounce)* bag frozen corn
(or 3-4 ears fresh corn cut off the cob)

2 Tablespoons olive oil

3 Tablespoons mayonnaise

3-4 ounces Cotija or feta cheese, crumbled

2 Tablespoons fresh lime juice

1 Tablespoon finely chopped jalapeño peppers

⅓ cup fresh finely chopped cilantro leaves

2 Tablespoons finely chopped red onion

2 cloves garlic, minced

½ teaspoons chili powder

Salt and pepper to taste

Add olive oil to a large skillet over medium heat. Add the corn and let cook until the corn starts to char. This will take 7-8 minutes and you need to stir the corn often while it cooks.

In a large bowl, mix together the mayonnaise, cheese, lime juice, peppers, cilantro, red onion, garlic, and chili powder. When the corn is done, fold it into the other ingredients. Taste for seasoning. Add salt and pepper to your taste. Serve immediately.

"This dish always adds a colorful, festive touch to any table!"
Krysta Shoults Coleman

BROCCOLI RIGATONI

Makes 8-10 servings

8 ounces rigatoni, cooked according to package directions and drained

8 slices Bear Creek Smokehouse® bacon, cut into 1" pieces

2 cups broccoli florets

2 cloves garlic, minced

2 cups shredded mozzarella cheese

¼ cup grated Parmesan cheese

⅛ teaspoon ground cayenne

¼ cup chopped fresh parsley leaves

Place the cooked rigatoni in a large bowl. Set aside.

In a 10" skillet, cook the bacon over medium heat until browned. Remove any unwanted drippings from the pan. Add the broccoli to the pan, stirring constantly until the broccoli is slightly tender. This will take 4-5 minutes. Add the garlic during the last 2 minutes. Stir the mixture into the cooked rigatoni. Set aside.

In a small bowl, blend the mozzarella with Parmesan cheese. (This will prevent clumping.) Add the cheeses to the broccoli mixture. Sprinkle in the cayenne. Taste for seasoning and add salt or more pepper if desired. Pour the mixture into a serving dish. Sprinkle the chopped parsley over the casserole before serving.

From the kitchen of Stacia Shoults

Be completely humble and gentle; be patient, bearing with one another in love.

Ephesians 4:2

BACON WRAPPED GREEN BEANS

Makes 10 servings

1 pound fresh green beans, ends removed

5 strips Bear Creek Smokehouse® bacon

3 Tablespoons butter

¼ cup brown sugar

1 clove garlic, minced or pressed through a garlic press

1 teaspoon soy sauce

"I love when Krysta invites us over for dinner 'cause I know she'll have these waitin' on me!"

Hunter Shoults

Krysta Shoults Coleman

If you enjoy oven roasted vegetables, skip to the next step. If you want the final product beans to be softer, boil or steam the green beans until tender/crisp. Drain. Set aside.

Fry or bake the bacon to partially cook. Do not cook until crisp. Place the bacon on paper towels to cool. Cut the strips in half using a scissors. Set aside.

Preheat the oven to 400 degrees.

Working with one piece of the bacon at a time, place 6-7 green beans crosswise on one strip of bacon. Wrap bacon around the beans to create a bundle. Secure the bacon with a toothpick. Place the bundle in a 13" x 9" oven-safe pan. (You can use a baking rack inside the pan to separate the bacon drippings and reduce fatty content.) Continue working the bacon and green beans in this manner until all the bacon is used. Set aside.

In a small saucepan, combine butter, brown sugar, garlic, and soy sauce. Heat until butter has melted and ingredients are blended. Brush or drizzle this mixture over the bundles. Bake 10-15 minutes or until heated throughout. Serve warm.

From the kitchen of Krysta Shoults Coleman

Be completely humble and gentle; be patient, bearing with one another in love.

Ephesians 4:2

BASIC PASTRY

Makes 1

2¼ cups flour, divided

¾ cup solid shortening

1 teaspoon salt

¼ cup cold water

Reserve ½ cup of the flour in a small bowl. Mix water into the flour to form a paste. Set aside.

Place remaining flour and salt in a large bowl. Cut shortening into flour with a pastry knife or with two knives making cutting motions through the flour. Mixture should resemble cornmeal consistency. Add the reserved flour paste to the flour / shortening mixture and stir until all the flour is incorporated. Turn dough onto a sheet of plastic wrap and wrap tightly. Store dough in refrigerator for one hour or until chilled. On clean, lightly floured surface, roll dough with rolling pin until ⅛" thick. Place in pie pan or follow the recipe you are creating for further directions.

"This is a fantastic Basic Pastry recipe that's been handed down for generations, in our family!"
Brenda Shoults

AMAZING COCONUT PIE

Makes 1 pie

2 cups milk

1 cup sugar

½ cup biscuit mix

4 eggs

¼ cup butter or margarine, softened

1½ teaspoons vanilla

1 cup coconut

Preheat oven to 350 degrees. Spray a pie pan with non-stick spray. Set aside.

In a blender, combine milk, sugar, biscuit mix, eggs, butter, and vanilla. Blend on low speed for two minutes. Pour into the prepared pie pan. Let stand for five minutes. Sprinkle the coconut evenly over the surface of the pie. Bake for 40 minutes or until set. Serve warm or cool.

Bee Bee's Sheet Cake

Serves 18

2 cups flour

2 cups sugar

2 sticks butter

2 Tablespoons cocoa powder

½ package German sweet chocolate

1 cup water

1 teaspoon baking soda

1 cup buttermilk

2 eggs

Icing:

1 stick butter

½ package German sweet chocolate

6 Tablespoons evaporated milk

2 Tablespoons cocoa powder

1 box confectioner's sugar

1 teaspoon vanilla

Chopped nuts, optional

Preheat oven to 400 degrees. Spray 10" x 15" x 1" cookie pan with non-stick spray. Set aside.

In a large bowl, sift flour and sugar together. Set aside.

In a medium sauce pan place butter, cocoa, German sweet chocolate, and water. Bring to boil *(only a boil)*, stir and pour over flour and sugar, mix well. Add buttermilk containing one teaspoon of baking soda. Then add two eggs beaten and mix well. Pour cocoa mixture into flour mixture. Stir well. Add buttermilk mixture while stirring. Pour mixture into prepared cookie pan and bake for 20 minutes or until it tests done. Remove from oven to cool slightly.

While cake is baking, prepare icing.

In a large saucepan heat butter, chocolate, milk, and cocoa. Bring to boil *(only a boil)*. Add one box confectioner's sugar *(more if necessary)*, one teaspoon vanilla and chopped nuts.

Frost cake while slightly warm. Sprinkle nuts over the frosting if desired.

From the kitchen of Brenda Shoults

He gives strength to the weary and increases the power of the weak.

Isaiah 40:29

CARROT CAKE

Serves 20

2 cups flour

2 teaspoons baking soda

2 teaspoons ground cinnamon

1 teaspoon salt

1¾ cups sugar

4 eggs

3 cups finely shredded carrots

1½ cups vegetable oil

2 teaspoons vanilla

Icing:

1 *(8 ounce)* package cream cheese, softened

1 pound *(small box)* confectioner's sugar

½ stick butter or margarine, softened

2 teaspoons vanilla

1 cup finely chopped walnuts or pecans

Preheat oven to 350 degrees. Grease and flour two 8" round cake pans. Set aside

In a large bowl, sift all dry ingredients together. Set aside.

In a medium bowl, mix liquid ingredients. Stir in carrots. Stir liquid ingredients into large bowl with dry ingredients. Mix to blend. Evenly divide mixture between the two prepared baking pans. Spread batter evenly in each pan. Bake 30 to 40 minutes or until cakes test done. Let cool.

For the icing: In a medium bowl, mix cream cheese and butter. Add vanilla. Mix in sugar and stir until smooth. Frost between layers and over the top and sides of cake.

Garnish cake with chopped nuts, if desired.

From the kitchen of Janie Watson

DID YOU KNOW?

Around the turn of the 19th century the Caddo Lake area of East Texas boomed with an influx of pearl hunters! Some were fortunate enough to find single pearls worth close to $1,000 in Caddo's fresh water mussels!

A colorful Japanese, George Murato, is said to have found more than $3,000 worth of pearls in a year! Later, when the pearl boom subsided, he shipped Caddo catfish eggs to a Midwest firm which packaged them as "Russian Caviar!"

"This Carrot Cake recipe of Janie's is one of the best I've ever had!"
Stacia Shoults

INDIAN WEDDING CAKE

Serves 18

2 cups sugar

2 cups flour

1 teaspoon soda

½ teaspoon salt

2 eggs

1 *(20 ounce)* can crushed pineapple

½ cup vegetable oil

1 teaspoon vanilla

Icing:

3½ cups powdered sugar

8 ounces cream cheese, softened

1 teaspoon vanilla

Preheat oven to 325 degrees. Spray a glass 13" x 9" baking pan with non-stick spray. Set aside.

In a large bowl, mix dry ingredients. Set aside.

In a medium bowl, mix oil, eggs, and vanilla. Stir in pineapple. Pour pineapple mixture into dry ingredients. Mix well to blend. Pour into prepared baking pan. Bake for 45 minutes or until cake tests done.

While cake is baking, prepare icing. Blend all ingredients.

Pour icing over the cake when it comes out of the oven and is still hot. Sprinkle chopped pecans over the icing if desired.

From the kitchen of Annette Belder

- BEAR BOTTOM TALL TALES BY BOBBY SHOULTS -

"We could never get the pilot light workin' in that ole' 8'x10' smokehouse! The way I'd do it is I'd get a piece of paper, turn the gas on, and light that piece of paper... then I'd throw that paper in there and run! It'd blow a fire out that door out there!

Another time I was up here a'cookin' some hot links. I had to leave for a while to go to a church league baseball game. Well, when I come back, boy them hot links were just right and juicy! When I went to roll' em out of the smokehouse, I had forgot to put the top bar in that kept 'em in place... Man-O-Man! They all just tumbled to the floor... I just 'bout cried!"

ITALIAN CREAM CHEESE CAKE

Serves 24

1 cup buttermilk

1 teaspoon baking soda

5 eggs, separated and at room temperature

1 stick butter or margarine, softened

2 cups sugar

2 cups flour

1 teaspoon vanilla

1 cup chopped pecans

1 *(4 ounce)* can shredded coconut

Cream Cheese Icing:

16 oz bag confectioner's sugar

8 ounces cream cheese, softened

½ stick butter or margarine, softened

2 teaspoons vanilla

"This Italian Cream Cheese Cake recipe of Dollie's is always a delight to serve to family or guests... and everyone always wants seconds!"
Stacia Shoults

Preheat oven to 350 degrees. Grease and flour three 9" cake pans. Set aside. In medium mixer bowl, whip egg whites until stiff peaks form. Set aside. Sift flour and baking soda together. Set aside.

In a large mixing bowl, cream butter with sugar. Add egg yolks one at a time, beating after each addition. Add ½ cup of the flour mixture to batter, mixing well. Add ⅓ of the buttermilk, mixing well Continue adding flour and buttermilk alternately mixing after each addition. Add ¼ of beaten egg whites gently stirring into batter by hand. Fold remaining egg whites into batter. Gently fold pecans and coconut into batter. Divide batter evenly between prepared cake pans. Bake for about 20 minutes or until cakes test done. Remove from oven and set on cake racks to cool for 10 minutes. Carefully remove cakes from pans and place them on waxed paper. Allow layers to cool.

In a large mixer bowl, combine cream cheese and butter. Mix on medium speed until well blended. Add vanilla and mix to blend. Add ⅓ of the bag of sugar. Mix on low speed to blend. Slowly add remaining sugar while mixing on low speed. When blended, beat on medium speed until smooth. Frost between the cake layers and assemble cake. Frost top and sides of cake. If desired, the cake sides can be decorated with chopped pecans.

From the kitchen of Dollie Dorsey Richardson

MARILYN'S HOMEMADE GLAZED DONUTS

Serves 6

1 container large buttermilk biscuits

Vegetable oil

2 cups confectioner's sugar

4 tablespoons milk

2 teaspoons vanilla extract

"These are my favorite donuts in the whole wide world! My mommy even lets me add food coloring to the icing. I like purple and pink donuts the best!"
Cooper Shoults

Prepare the glaze first by mixing the confectioner's sugar, milk, and vanilla extract. Set aside.

In a large saucepan or skillet, add vegetable oil to a depth of 2". Place over medium-high heat until oil reaches 325 degrees. While oil is heating, lay biscuits on a clean cutting board. Using a biscuit cutter or a small round cookie cutter, remove the center of each biscuit. *(These centers can also be fried.)* Carefully drop one or two donuts into the hot oil and cook until the bottoms are golden brown. Flip the donuts over to cook the other side. When golden brown, remove the donuts to a baking sheet lined with paper towels to drain. Repeat until all donuts are cooked. Toss the donuts in the reserved glaze and place on a wire rack to set the glaze. Serve while warm.

CARAMEL

Makes 2 Cups

1⅓ cups sugar

⅔ cup brown sugar

½ cup butter

⅔ cup Pet® milk

1 teaspoon vanilla

In a heavy saucepan, heat all ingredients except vanilla over low heat, stirring constantly. Continue cooking until mixture reaches soft ball stage or 235 degrees on a candy thermometer. *(This step takes 15-18 minutes.)* Let cool slightly. Beat in the vanilla to blend well. Let mixture cool before serving on cake or ice cream.

From the kitchen of Juanice Shoults

NELLIE'S PUDDING CAKE

Serves 18

1½ cups flour

1½ sticks butter or margarine

1½ cups chopped nuts *(pecans or walnuts)*

1 *(8 ounce)* package cream cheese, softened

1 cup powdered sugar

1 *(8 ounce)* container of Cool Whip®

1 *(8 ounce)* can crushed pineapple, juice reserved

2 *(3.4 ounce)* packages instant vanilla pudding mix

2½ cups milk

Shredded coconut, to taste

Preheat oven to 350 degrees.

In a small saucepan over low heat, melt butter. Stir in flour and nuts. Pour mixture into 9" x 13" baking dish. Spread evenly over bottom of dish and press flat to form a bottom crust. Bake for 20 minutes. Set aside to cool. In a medium bowl, mix cream cheese, powdered sugar and one cup of Cool Whip®. Mix in drained pineapple and pour mixture over cooled crust.
Set aside.

In a medium mixer bowl, mix instant pudding with milk. Add reserved pineapple juice. Mix on medium speed with mixer for about two minutes. Pour pudding mixture over cream cheese layer in baking dish. Top with remaining Cool Whip®. Sprinkle generously with coconut if desired. Cover and refrigerate to store for up to one week.

"This Pudding Cake recipe of Nellie's has been a family favorite for generations! It's just as good now as it was decades ago!"
Brenda Shoults

PUMPKIN SWIRL CHEESECAKE

Serves 12

2 cups vanilla wafer crumbs

¼ cup butter, melted

2 *(8 ounce)* packages cream cheese, softened

¾ cup sugar

1 teaspoon vanilla

3 eggs

1 cup canned pumpkin

¾ teaspoon ground cinnamon

¼ teaspoon ground or grated nutmeg

"My mother, Muriel, always made this for us on Thanksgiving. However, my sisters and I could eat this anytime of the year because it's just that good!"
Tracy Shoults

Preheat oven to 350 degrees. Place crumbs in zip-lock bag. Drizzle butter into the crumbs. Zip bag shut and shake until butter is evenly distributed. Press crumbs into bottom and sides of a spring-form pan. Set aside.

In a mixing bowl, combine cream cheese, ½ cup sugar, and vanilla. Mix on medium speed until well blended. Add eggs, one at a time, beating well after each one is added. Reserve one cup of this mixture for later use. Add pumpkin, remaining sugar and spices to mixer bowl. Mix well. Pour half of the pumpkin mixture into the crumb crust. Carefully add reserved cream cheese mixture over the pumpkin mixture to form a layer. Top with remaining pumpkin mixture. Drag a knife through the batter to create a marble effect. Bake for 50-55 minutes or until set. Remove from oven and let cool 15 minutes. Release sides of cake from pan. Cool for additional 30 minutes. Chill cake before serving.

From the kitchen of Karen Gasper

PEANUT PATTIES

Makes 36 Patties

3 cups sugar

1 cup light corn syrup

½ cup water

3 cups raw peanuts

1 stick butter or margarine

1 teaspoon vanilla

Red food coloring, if desired

Place first four ingredients in large saucepan. Bring to a boil and set timer for five minutes exactly. Remove from heat. Add remaining ingredients.

Beat the mixture by hand for approximately 15 minutes. Place wax paper or baking parchment on flat kitchen surface. One spoonful at a time, deposit peanut mixture onto the paper. Let cool. Place patties in airtight container to store.

From the kitchen of Janie Watson

CHOCOLATE FUDGE

Makes approximately 12-16 pieces

3 cups sugar

3 Tablespoons + 1 teaspoon cocoa powder

3 Tablespoons light corn syrup

Dash salt

1 cup evaporated milk

1 teaspoon vanilla

2 Tablespoons butter

Butter a 9" x 9" glass dish. Set aside.

Fill a large metal bowl ½ full of ice cubes. Set aside.

In a large heavy saucepan, cook all ingredients, stirring often until it reaches the soft ball stage or 235 degrees on a candy thermometer. Remove the pan from heat and set into the bowl of ice cubes. Stir often until the mixture has cooled. Pour the chocolate mixture into the prepared glass dish. Let chill before cutting into serving pieces. Store the fudge in an airtight container in the refrigerator.

From the kitchen of Janie Watson

PRALINE THUMBPRINT COOKIES

Makes 2 dozen

1 cup butter, softened

1 cup powdered sugar, sifted

2 cups flour, sifted

1 cup finely chopped pecans

1 teaspoon vanilla

Filling:

½ cup butter or margarine

1 cup brown sugar, firmly pack to measure

½ cup evaporated milk

2 cups powdered sugar

½ teaspoon vanilla

"They don't call me 'Cupcake' around here for nothing... I love sweets and this recipe from Anita is one of my absolute favorites!"
Stacia Shoults

Preheat oven to 375 degrees.

In a medium bowl, cream butter. Add vanilla. Gradually add powdered sugar beating well on medium speed with mixer. Slowly add flour while mixing. Stir in pecans. Roll mixture into balls the size of walnuts and put them not-touching on ungreased cookie sheet. Press thumb in the center of each ball to make an indentation. Bake cookies for 15 to 17 minutes or until golden brown. Set aside to cool.

For the filling: In a medium saucepan, melt butter. Add sugar. Bring to simmer stirring constantly for two minutes. Gradually stir in milk while stirring. Bring to simmer for about two minutes or until a candy thermometer reads 232 degrees. Remove from heat and cool until mixture is luke warm. Stir in powdered sugar and vanilla. With a wooden spoon, beat mixture until smooth. Fill each cookie indentation with the mixture.

From the kitchen of Anita Overhultz

DID YOU KNOW?

Bear Creek Smokehouse is a great place to 'hunker down' for the Shoults family, Bear Creek employees, and many neighbors that live on or near the Shoults family farm! The building itself is built like a bunker... constructed mostly of concrete and steel, surviving a direct tornado hit during the busy holiday season back in December, 1983! It's quite a comfort knowing you can ride out the severe storms and tornadoes that occasionally rip through the area, in a shelter that smells this awesome!

Peach Cobbler

Serves 6-8

1⅓ cups flour

½ teaspoon salt

½ cup + 1 Tablespoon solid shortening

3 Tablespoons cold water

2-3 large cans sliced peaches, drained, reserving 1 cup of the liquids

1 cup of sugar

1 stick of butter

**See below for fresh peach directions*

"Nothing says summer to me, more than a bowl of fresh Peach Cobbler with a big ole' dollop of homemade ice cream!"

Robbie Shoults

Preheat oven to 425 degrees.

Place flour and salt in large bowl. Using a pastry blender, cut the shortening into the flour until it resembles coarse corn meal texture. With a fork, stir in cold water and form into a ball. Place the dough ball on a sheet of plastic wrap. Wrap dough tightly and refrigerate while working with peaches.

If using canned peaches, place the peaches and reserved liquid in a Pyrex® baking dish. Sprinkle the peaches with one cup of sugar. Cut a stick of butter into ½ tablespoon pats. Place the butter pats evenly over the surface of the sugared peaches. Set aside. Lightly flour a clean kitchen worksurface. Place chilled dough on the surface and roll with a rolling pin until it is ¼" thick. Using a pizza cutter or sharp knife, cut the dough into 1" wide strips. Lay the strips in a crisscross pattern over the peaches in the baking pan. Bake for 30 minutes. Remove from oven and sprinkle crust strips with a little sugar. Return to the oven for 10 minutes. Remove from oven and let cool slightly before serving.

If you are using fresh peaches: Peel and remove pits from 2-3 pounds of fresh peaches. Cut peaches into slices and put in a large saucepan or kettle. Add 3 cups sugar, 1½ sticks butter, and ⅔ cup water to the peaches. Bring to simmer and cook until peaches are soft. Let cool slightly before proceeding with cobbler instructions.

Sopapilla Cheesecake

Serves 18

2 cans Pillsbury® Crescents

2 cups sugar *(divided)*

3 *(8 ounce)* packages cream cheese, softened

1½ teaspoons vanilla

1 stick butter, melted

1 teaspoon ground cinnamon

"This south-of-the-border dessert always reminds me of the flavors of Mexico! I think the adults enjoy it just as much as the kids do!"

Tracy Shoults

Preheat oven to 350 degrees. Spray a 9" x 13" baking pan with non-stick spray. Set aside.

Roll out one can of crescent rolls and place in bottom of baking pan. Press gently to close any gaps in the dough. Set aside.

In a mixer bowl, blend cream cheese, 1½ cups sugar, and vanilla until smooth. Spread cream cheese mixture evenly over dough in baking pan. Set aside. On working surface, roll out the remaining can of crescent rolls. Place over cream cheese mixture. Pour melted butter evenly over the dough.

Put remaining ½ cup sugar in small bowl and stir in cinnamon. Sprinkle sugar mixture evenly over the buttered dough. Bake for 30-35 minutes or until slightly browned. Let cool before serving. Cover tightly and refrigerate to store.

- Rememberin' Bear Bottom By Hunter Shoults -

"We've always loved livin' close. We all live near each other, even still to this day!

I used to hop on my little four-wheeler and dad would watch me till I got to the top of the hill behind our house and BeeBee would be on the other side of the hill to watch me go down!

I loved ridin' over to BeeBee's 'cause she always had somethin' good to eat!

Now, I drive my family over the hill to BeeBee's where we all eat on the back porch, just like we used to!"

ORANGE SLICE CAKE

As seen on page 157, Serves 8

1 cup butter or margarine, softened

2 cups sugar

4 eggs

2½ cups flour

2 Tablespoons grated orange rind, fresh not dried, divided

1 teaspoon baking soda

1 cup buttermilk

1 pound dates, seeds removed

2 cups chopped pecans

1 pound orange slice candy

2 cups shredded coconut

Glaze:

2 cups powdered sugar

1 cup orange juice

Remaining 1 Tablespoon orange rind

Preheat oven to 275 degrees. Grease and flour a Bundt pan or tube cake pan. Set aside.

Stir baking soda into buttermilk. Set aside.

In a food processor with metal blade, mix ½ cup of the sugar, pecans, one Tablespoon grated orange rind, dates, and orange slice candy. Pulse until finely chopped. Stir in coconut. Set aside.

In a large bowl, mix remaining sugar, flour, eggs, butter, and buttermilk mixture. Beat well with hand mixer until well blended. Add orange slice mixture. Stir to blend evenly. Pour into prepared Bundt pan. Bake for two hours or until cake tests done. While cake is baking, prepare glaze. Mix the ingredients until smooth.

When cake tests done, remove from oven and let it stand five minutes. If necessary, run a knife around pan edges to loosen the cake. Pour glaze over the cake slowly. When cake has cooled, invert the pan and remove the cake. Refrigerate before serving. *(This cake freezes well.)*

From the kitchen of Mrs. Bessie Smith

DID YOU KNOW?

Hick and Nellie Shoults' business phone number was 5995!
This original number is still used today in the form of 903. 935. 5995, one of the Bear Creek Smokehouse business phone extensions!

BREAD PUDDING

Makes 8-10 servings

8 slices white bread broken into large pieces

¼ teaspoon ground or freshly grated nutmeg

½ teaspoon ground cinnamon

1 ½ quarts whole milk

5 eggs

1 teaspoon vanilla

¾ cup sugar

4 Tablespoons cold butter cut into slices

⅓ cup golden or dark raisins

Preheat oven to 375 degrees. Spray a 2 quart baking dish with non-stick spray. Distribute the bread pieces evenly in the prepared baking dish. Sprinkle with raisins. Set aside.

In a large mixer bowl, beat the eggs with sugar until mixture is lemon color. With mixer on low speed, add milk in a thin stream. Stir in vanilla. Add cinnamon and nutmeg. Slowly pour milk mixture over the bread pieces. Lay butter slices over the top of the mixture distributing evenly. Bake for 40-45 minutes or until set and lightly browned on top.

DATE BALLS

Makes approximately 2 dozen candies

⅓ cup butter, melted

½ cup sugar

1 package pitted chopped dates

2 cups Rice Krispies® cereal

½ cup finely chopped pecans

"This Date Ball recipe is not only appetizing, but an easy-to-make favorite sweet treat for the family!"
Brenda Shoults

Line a baking sheet with waxed paper. Set aside.

Distribute the chopped pecans on a dinner plate or in a pie plate. Set aside.

In a medium size bowl, stir together sugar, melted butter, and dates. Stir in rice cereal. Form the mixture into walnut size balls and roll each date ball in the chopped pecans. Place the date balls not touching on the waxed paper. Let the balls come to room temperature before storing in an airtight container.

CHOCOLATE DELIGHT

Makes 16 servings

1 cup flour

1 cup butter, at room temperature

1 cup chopped pecans or walnuts

8 ounces cream cheese, at room temperature

1 cup confectioner's sugar

1 container Cool Whip®, divided

4½ cups milk

1 small package instant vanilla pudding

2 small packages instant chocolate pudding

Chocolate bar, grated for topping

Preheat oven to 325 degrees. Spray a 9" x 13" casserole dish with non-stick spray. Set aside. In a mixer bowl, combine flour, butter, and chopped nuts. Mix until blended. Pour the dough into the prepared dish. Spread the mixture evenly in the pan and pat down to form a crust on the bottom of the dish. Bake 15-20 minutes or until light golden brown. Set aside to cool. In a mixer bowl, combine cream cheese, confectioner's sugar, and one cup of the Cool Whip®. When combined, pour the mixture over the cooled crust. Set aside.

In a mixer bowl, combine the milk and pudding mixes. Mix to blend. Spread the pudding mixture over the cream cheese layer. Top the pudding layer with the remaining Cool Whip® and garnish with the grated chocolate bar. Cover with plastic wrap and chill overnight before serving.

- REMEMBERIN' BEAR BOTTOM BY HUNTER SHOULTS -

"The first time I got to go fishin' in cypress, dad baited my hook with the worm and cork and I didn't even know how to cast. I was so little, but I threw it out there anyhow and that 'ole worm managed to find the water! Low and behold, that fish up and jumped on my hook, soon as it hit the water... my first cast ever and I caught a fish!!

That was a special lucky spot to fish in... my dad, grandfather, and great grandfather have all fished in that very spot and now I take my kids there!"

FROSTED CARAMEL SQUARES

Serves 12

½ cup vegetable shortening

1 cup sugar

2 eggs

½ teaspoon vanilla

½ teaspoon salt

1 teaspoon baking powder

1½ cups flour

Topping:

1 egg white

1 cup light brown sugar

½ teaspoon vanilla

½ cup nuts, chopped fine

Preheat oven to 325 degrees. Grease and flour a baking pan or cookie sheet with 1" sides. Set aside.

In a mixer bowl, cream shortening. Add sugar gradually to the shortening. Add eggs one at a time to the mixture while mixer is on low. Add vanilla. Mix to blend.

In a large bowl, sift together dry ingredients. Add gradually to shortening mixture while mixer is on low. Mix to blend. Spread mixture evenly over surface of prepared cookie sheet. Set aside.

For topping: In a small mixer bowl, beat the egg white until soft peaks form. Fold in brown sugar. Mix in vanilla. Set aside.

Finely chop nuts or shred coconut to taste. Sprinkle mixture in baking pan with nuts or coconut. Spread egg white mixture evenly over nuts or coconut mixture. Bake for 20 to 30 minutes or until lightly browned on top. Cut into squares. Cool before serving or storing in airtight container.

"MeMaw used to make these for Bobby. They have always been his favorite. Now, I make them for him on special occasions!"

Brenda Shoults

DID YOU KNOW?

Around 1960, Bear Creek Smokehouse printed its first catalog, offering smoked turkeys and chickens packaged and shipped for the Thanksgiving & Christmas season! The business has continued to expand!

Today, with Catalogs, Website, Social Media & Email Marketing, Bear Creek Smokehouse has grown to the point that a wide variety of delicious smoked gourmet selections are now smoked and shipped year 'round!

All with the daily careful attention to quality and detail, by the Shoults Family!

CHOCOLATE CREAM PIE

Serves 8

9" Baked pie shell

1½ cups sugar

½ teaspoon salt

2½ Tablespoons cornstarch

1 Tablespoon flour

2 cups milk

1½ cups whipping cream

2 squares unsweetened baking chocolate, cut into small pieces

1½ squares sweetened chocolate, cut into small pieces

3 egg yolks at room temperature

1 Tablespoon butter

1½ teaspoons vanilla

Meringue

3 egg whites at room temperature

¼ teaspoon cream of tartar

3 Tablespoons sugar

Put the egg yolks in a small bowl and beat with a fork or whisk to blend. Set aside.

Preheat the oven to 400 degrees.

Combine sugar, salt, cornstarch, and flour in a large saucepan. Stir well. Place saucepan over medium heat. Stir in milk and cream while stirring constantly. Add chocolate. Continue stirring until mixture thickens and simmers for one minute. Remove from heat. Slowly stir a small amount of the chocolate mixture into the egg yolks. Blend the egg yolk/chocolate into the hot mixture and let boil one minute, stirring constantly. Remove from heat and add butter and vanilla. Mix well. Continue stirring to blend and set aside.

Prepare meringue in a clean bowl. Mix eggs, cream of tartar, and sugar. Beat with a clean whisk or electric mixer until soft peaks form. Set aside. Pour the warm chocolate filling into prepared pie shell. Spoon whipped egg whites over chocolate filling and gently spread to cover the surface of the pie. The egg whites should be touching the crust. Create peaks in the egg whites by touching the top surface of the egg whites with the back of a large spoon or spatula and pulling straight up. Place the pie in the oven and cook 10 minutes or until the meringue is lightly browned.

From the kitchen of Dorothy Skeans

Julia Child & Dorothy Skeans

Hunter's Favorite Cookies

Makes about 48 cookies

1 cup butter, at room temperature

1 cup sugar

½ cup packed brown sugar

1 egg

1 teaspoon fresh orange zest

2 Tablespoons orange juice

2 ½ cups flour

½ teaspoon baking soda

½ teaspoon salt

2 cups chopped cranberries

½ cup chopped walnuts or almonds

Frosting:

½ teaspoon orange zest

3 Tablespoons orange juice

1½ cups confectioner's sugar

Preheat oven to 375 degrees. Sift together the flour, baking soda, and salt. Set aside.

In a large mixer bowl, cream together the butter, white sugar, and brown sugar until smooth. Add the egg and beat until well blended. Mix in the orange zest and orange juice. Add the flour mixture and mix until blended. Stir in the cranberries and nuts. Mix until incorporated into the dough. Drop the dough by rounded tablespoons onto an ungreased cookie sheet about 2" apart. Bake 12-14 minutes or until the edges are golden. Remove the cookies to a wire rack to cool.

In a small bowl, mix the frosting ingredients until smooth. Use this mixture to frost the tops of the baked cookies.

Robbie Shoults

- Bear Bottom Tall Tales By Bobby Shoults -

"It was a hoot when the schools came out to look at the turkeys... they'd never seen turkeys before. We were the first in the county to raise turkeys! They thought that was the best field trip they'd ever been on! We'd give them a hat and stick a feather in it. That was in the 50's and 60's!"

CHRISTMAS COOKIES

Makes approximately 4 dozen cookies

1 cup shortening

2 cups sugar

4 eggs

2 Tablespoons heavy cream

4 cups flour

⅛ teaspoon salt

4 teaspoons baking powder

1 teaspoon vanilla

"The Christmas Holiday Season is always a very special time in Bear Bottom! These fun Christmas Cookies make it even more special!"
Brenda Shoults

Sift the flour, salt, and baking powder together. Set aside. In large mixing bowl, mix shortening and sugar until well combined. One at a time, add eggs, beating after each addition.

Add the heavy cream. Add the vanilla and mix.

Add one cup of flour mixture and mix on low speed to incorporate into shortening mixture. Continue adding one cup of flour and mixing after each addition.

Mold dough into a ball shape. Wrap with plastic wrap and place in refrigerator to chill for about a half hour. Preheat oven to 400 degrees. Spray two cookie sheets with non-stick spray. Set aside. On a lightly floured clean kitchen work surface, place unwrapped dough ball. With a butter knife, cut dough in half.

Wrap one half of dough in plastic wrap and store in refrigerator until needed. Working with a lightly floured rolling pin, roll dough to ³/₈" thick. Cut into shapes with Christmas cookie cutters. To prevent dough from sticking to the cookie cutters, before cutting each cookie, briefly dip the edges of the cutter into flour. Place cut-out cookies on prepared cookie sheet and bake until lightly brown. This will take 8-10 minutes. When dough is all cut, repeat the process with remaining dough ball from refrigerator. As cookies are removed from oven, using a cookie spatula, carefully transfer them to a clean sheet of waxed paper or a wire cookie rack. Let cookies cool to room temperature before frosting.

GEORGE E. KENNEDY'S FUDGE

Makes approximately 16 pieces

1½ cups sugar

2½ Tablespoons cocoa

⅛ teaspoon salt

2 Tablespoons light corn syrup

½ cup milk

2 Tablespoons butter

1 teaspoon vanilla

1 cup chopped pecans

"My grandfather loved making fudge... So much so that he even made a living doing it!"
Stacia Shoults

Butter a 9" x 9" glass dish. Set aside.

In a small saucepan, mix sugar, cocoa, and salt. Stir in corn syrup and milk. Cook over medium-low heat, stirring gently but constantly.

The mixture should boil gently for about 50 minutes or until it tests 240 degrees using a candy thermometer. Remove from heat and add butter, vanilla and pecans. Immediately pour into the prepared glass dish. Set aside to cool to room temperature. Cut into bite sized squares to serve.

CREAM CHEESE POUND CAKE

Makes 1 cake

3 cups sugar

3 sticks butter or margarine, softened

6 eggs

1 teaspoon lemon extract

1 teaspoon vanilla extract

1 *(8 ounce)* package cream cheese, softened

3 cups flour, sifted

Preheat oven to 325 degrees. Spray a Bundt pan with non-stick spray. Set aside. In a large mixer bowl, combine sugar and butter. Mix until well blended. Add eggs one at a time, beating after each addition. Add extracts and cream cheese then beat until smooth. One cup at a time, add flour to mixture beating after each addition. Pour batter into prepared pan and bake for 1 hour and 10 minutes or until cake tests done. Remove from oven and allow cake to cool for 10 minutes. Carefully invert cake onto a wire rack and remove Bundt pan. Let cake cool. Dust cake with confectioner's sugar if desired.

HELLO DOLLY COOKIES

Makes approximately 20 cookies

1 stick butter or margarine, melted

1 cup graham cracker crumbs

1 cup Eagle Brand® milk or condensed milk

6 ounces chocolate chips

1 cup chopped nuts

1 cup shredded coconut

1 teaspoon vanilla

"These melt-in-your-mouth Hello Dolly Cookies combine the decadent flavors of chocolate, coconut and Eagle Brand Milk, to create this irresistible dessert!"
Stacia Shoults

Preheat oven to 325 degrees. Spray a 13" x 9" glass baking dish with non-stick spray. Set aside.

Put cracker crumbs into a zip top bag. Drizzle melted butter into bag. Close bag and gently rock it from side-to-side to evenly distribute butter. Pour crumbs into prepared baking dish. Cover with a piece of waxed paper and press evenly over bottom of pan to create a crust. Remove waxed paper. Set pan aside.

Add vanilla to condensed milk. Drizzle ½ of the mixture over crust. Evenly distribute nuts, coconut, and chocolate chips over the crust. Drizzle with the remaining condensed milk. Bake for 25-30 minutes or until top surface and edges are lightly browned. Cool before cutting into serving pieces.

DUMP CAKE

Servings 18

1 large can crushed pineapple with juice

1 can cherry pie filling

1 box white or yellow cake mix

½ stick butter or margarine, melted

¾ cup chopped pecans

Preheat oven to 350 degrees. Spray a 9" x 13" baking dish with non-stick spray. Evenly distribute the pineapple and cherry pie filling in the baking dish. Distribute the dry cake mix over the fruit layer. Evenly distribute the chopped nuts over the cake mix. Drizzle the melted butter evenly over the cake surface. Bake for 40-45 minutes or until the cake tests done. Set aside to cool before serving.

From the kitchen of Glenda Dorsey

ANITA'S UPSIDE DOWN CAKE

Serves 18

1 cup shredded coconut

1 cup chopped pecans

1 box cake mix

2 sticks butter or margarine, melted

8 ounces cream cheese, softened

1 box confectioner's sugar

"This Upside Down Cake of Anita's is simply melt-in-your-mouth good!"
Brenda Shoults

Preheat oven to 350 degrees. Spray a 9" x 13" baking dish with non-stick spray. Evenly distribute coconut and pecans over the bottom surface of the baking dish. Set aside.

Prepare the cake mix according to package directions. Pour the cake batter evenly distributing over the coconut and pecans. Set aside.

In a mixing bowl, combine cream cheese with butter. Mix in the confectioner's sugar until smooth. Pour over the cake batter. Bake for 35-40 minutes or until cake tests done.

CHOCOLATE FUDGE SAUCE

Serves 4

1 square baking chocolate

1 stick butter or margarine

⅛ teaspoon salt

3 cups sugar

1 large can Pet® evaporated milk

Use a double boiler to make this recipe. Bring the water in the bottom pan to a simmer. In the top pan, add the butter and chocolate. Cook until melted. Add salt. Gradually add the sugar, stirring to blend. Stir in the milk and cook until heated through.

To serve, drizzle over some homemade vanilla ice cream on a hot day!

From the kitchen of Wanda Todd

Now may the Lord of peace himself give you peace at all times and in every way....

2 Thessalonians 3:16

"When the Longhorns start grazing
in a pasture full of beautiful Coreopsis,
it signals that mid-summer has arrived!"

Robbie Shoults

GOLDEN'S COOKIE

Makes approximately 20 cookies

1 stick butter or margarine, melted

1 box cake mix

4 eggs, divided

8 ounces cream cheese, softened

1 box confectioner's sugar

1 cup shredded coconut

½ teaspoon vanilla

Preheat oven to 350 degrees. Spray a 13" x 9" glass baking dish with non-stick spray. Set aside.

In a large mixing bowl, stir butter into cake mix. Add one egg and stir well to blend ingredients. Put mixture into the prepared baking dish. Cover with waxed paper and press evenly to form a crust over the bottom surface of pan. Set aside.

In a large mixing bowl, blend the remaining three eggs into the softened cream cheese. Stir in confectioner's sugar until well blended. Add coconut and vanilla stirring to blend. Pour this mixture over crust. Distribute evenly. Bake for 30-35 minutes or until top surface is lightly browned. Let cool before cutting into serving pieces.

From the kitchen of Wilma Dorsey Stracner

- BEAR BOTTOM RAMBLINGS BY ROBBIE SHOULTS -

"Hunting and fishing have been a vital part of man's existence since the good Lord placed us in this world thousands of years ago!

These are also sports that every generation of the Shoults boys have enjoyed for decades!

The Shoults' land has always been teeming with an abundance of whitetail deer, ducks, squirrels, hogs, an occasional flock of geese and, back in the day when we were farming, my dad said he could always get his limit of bobwhite quail and the Little Cypress Creek was full of just about every kind of fish imaginable!

Makes me thankful to be blessed with an appreciation for the wildlife of Bear Bottom"

HEAVENLY HASH

Makes 8-10 servings

1 cup pineapple chunks, or crushed pineapple, drained

3 apples, cored and diced

1 cup miniature marshmallows *(or 12 regular size marshmallows cut into quarters)*

⅔ cup heavy cream

2 Tablespoons sugar

1 egg

½ cup sugar

1 teaspoon flour

⅓ cup distilled or apple vinegar

⅓ cup water

Use a double boiler to complete a portion of this recipe. In the top pan, mix the egg with ½ cup sugar and flour, stirring well to blend. Add the vinegar and water. Place the top pan over the bottom pan and bring water in the bottom pan to a simmer. Stir the sugar mixture constantly with a whisk. Cook until thickened. Remove the top pan and set aside to cool.

In a mixer bowl, beat cream with two Tablespoons sugar until it reaches soft peaks. Set aside.

In a large bowl, mix pineapple, apples, and marshmallows. Stir in the cooled sugar mixture and mix until evenly distributed. Fold in the whipped cream. Chill. Serve cold.

From the kitchen of Mama Dorsey

PECAN PIE

Serves 8

1 (9") pie shell

1 cup sugar

½ cup light Karo® syrup

3 eggs, beaten

1 stick butter, melted

1 cup pecan halves or pieces

Preheat oven to 350 degrees.

In a large bowl, mix the sugar, syrup, and eggs. Stir in the melted butter. Mix until blended. Add the pecans. Pour into the pie shell and bake for 55 minutes or until the crust is golden brown.

From the kitchen of Mary Ann Whyte

GERMAN CHOCOLATE CAKE

Serves 6-8

1 package Baker's® German Chocolate

½ cup water

1 cup vegetable shortening or butter

2 cups sugar

4 eggs, separated and at room temperature

½ teaspoon salt

1 teaspoon vanilla

2½ cups cake flour

1 teaspoon baking soda

1 cup buttermilk

Filling and Icing:

1½ cups sugar

2 Tablespoons flour

1½ cups milk

½ cup butter or margarine

1 cup flaked coconut

½ cup chopped pecans

Double these amounts if you want thicker coverage for icing and filling.

"This German Chocolate Cake Recipe has been handed down through the generations in our family! It's always a special treat around the Christmas Holidays!"
Brenda Shoults

Preheat oven to 350 degrees. Grease and flour three *(8" or 9")* pans. Line bottom of each pan with greased waxed paper, cut to fit. Set pans aside. In small saucepan on low heat, melt chocolate in water. Set aside to cool. Sift cake flour, salt, and soda together. Set aside. Beat egg whites until they form stiff peaks. Set aside. In a large mixer bowl, cream shortening and sugar until fluffy. One at a time, add egg yolks beating after each addition. Add cooled chocolate and vanilla and mix to blend. With mixer on low, add about ⅓ of flour mixture gradually. Pour in ⅓ of buttermilk and mix to blend. Continue adding flour and buttermilk in this manner. When all flour and buttermilk are incorporated, remove mixer. Using a spatula, fold in beaten egg whites. Divide mixture evenly in three prepared pans. Bake 35-40 minutes or until cakes test done. Remove from oven and cool on wire racks for 10 minutes before removing cakes from pans. Gently peel away waxed paper. Let cakes cool before assembly.

To prepare icing: In a medium saucepan, stir sugar and flour together to blend. Stir in milk and heat to simmer while stirring constantly. When mixture begins to boil, add butter, nuts, and coconut. Simmer filling for seven minutes stirring constantly. Remove from heat. Stir the mixture as it cools. When mixture reaches a workable temperature, spread small amount evenly over tops of cake layers. Assemble layers, lining up edges. Use remaining mixture to cover sides of cake. Additional coconut and chopped pecans may be used to garnish.

From the kitchen of Nellie Shoults

NITA'S PRALINES

Makes approximately 2 dozen pralines

1½ cups brown sugar

½ cup sugar

3 Tablespoons light corn syrup

6 Tablespoons milk

1 stick butter or margarine

2 cups pecan halves or pieces

2 Tablespoons vanilla

Place a sheet of waxed paper on a clean kitchen work surface or cookie sheet. Set aside.

In a large heavy saucepan over medium-high heat, cook brown sugar, sugar, corn syrup, milk, and butter. Stir often and cook until mixture reaches the soft ball stage or reads 235 degrees on a candy thermometer. Stir in nuts and vanilla. Using a tablespoon, drop the mixture onto the waxed paper. Let cool before storing in an airtight container.

OATMEAL COOKIES

Makes 3-4 dozen cookies

1 box spice cake mix

2 cups rolled oats

2 eggs

⅔ cup vegetable oil

½ cup milk

2 cups raisins

1 cup either chopped nuts or shredded coconut *(both if desired)*

¼ cup brown sugar

Preheat oven to 350 degrees. Set out a baking pan or cookie sheet. Do not spray or grease the pan.

In a large mixing bowl, blend the cake mix, brown sugar, and oats. Set aside.

In a small bowl, beat the eggs until frothy. Add the vegetable oil and milk. Stir until well blended. Add the liquid ingredients to the dry ingredients and stir until well blended. Stir in the raisins, nuts and/or coconut. Drop the dough by heaping spoonfuls onto the cookie sheet leaving 2" between to allow for spreading. Bake about 12 minutes or until golden browned.

From the kitchen of Nancy Shoults Palmer

SNICKER® CINNA'MORES

Serves 4-6

1 bag of fun size Snicker® bars

1 bag of large marshmallows

2 pkgs cinnamon graham crackers

"When you crave S'mores but don't have the ingredients, you have to improvise... these are better!"

Shae McDonald

Place Snicker® bar and marshmallow on cinnamon graham cracker. Top with another cinnamon graham cracker. Place in microwave-safe dish.

Melt in microwave on high power for 15 seconds.

Serve warm.

From the kitchen of Shae McDonald

Shae McDonald

- BEAR BOTTOM TALL TALES BY BOBBY SHOULTS -

"Back in the early days, when times were tough, I'd take a crew out to the creek when it was low in the summer. We'd muddy the potholes with a hoe, then scoop up the fish with dip nets as they came up to the surface for air! Not sure if that was legal, even in Bear Bottom, back in the day!

Our huntin' hasn't always been limited just to Bear Bottom though! My dad used to take a whole group of friends out in an ole' school bus, converted into a huntin' camper!

They'd load up that ole' school bus and a'head out to Wyomin' on an annual huntin' trip ev'ry year! One year, when I was still in high school, back in the 50's, I got to go with 'em!

That year I got a Bear and an Elk, while everyone else came home empty-handed! I was all excited, but man-o-man did that ever make for a long trip back home! Not a soul would speak to me the whole way back to Texas!

And I ain't lived it down to this day neither... I still get kidded 'bout it, now and again!"

Peanut Butter Cups

Makes approximately 16 candies

2 sticks butter or margarine, melted or softened

1 cup graham cracker crumbs

1 box confectioner's sugar

1 cup chunky peanut butter

1 large package chocolate chips, melted

Spray a 9" x 9" glass pan with non-stick spray (or rub with butter to coat the pan). Set aside. To a large mixing bowl, add the graham cracker crumbs, confectioner's sugar, peanut butter, and butter. Mix the ingredients using your clean or gloved hands. Pour into the prepared glass pan. Place a piece of waxed paper over the mixture and using the flat of your palms or the back of a large spoon, press the mixture to form an even crust. Pour the melted chocolate over the crust layer. Refrigerate until chilled and cut into serving pieces.

- Bear Bottom Ramblings By Robbie Shoults -

"My daughter-in-law, Stacia, and I have a very special relationship, constantly trying to keep each other 'in check' and in touch with reality! Therefore, I've found it necessary to rename her so she, nor anyone else, shall ever forget the story I'm about to tell!

You see, I sent our ever-faithful Mike Whyte to Dallas, in a one-ton truck with a large cargo trailer, expecting him to carry out the tough mission and return in a timely fashion! Five hours after he was due, I began to worry!

About that time, Mike appears with a disgusted look saying... 'Oh Lord, we got Cupcakes!' You see, Stacia had instructed Mike to pick up a dozen 'high-dollar', Red Velvet Cupcakes from some specialty bakery in downtown Dallas!

I still kid her about Mike spending hours dragging a huge trailer through Dallas, to get the most expensive Cupcakes E-V-E-R! I did try one though and it was delicious, but don't tell 'Cupcake'!"

MINCEMEAT PIE

Makes 1 pie

1 (9") deep dish pie crust

1 (9") pie crust, for the pie top

1 package None Such® mincemeat

2 cups water

1¼ cups sugar, divided

¼ cup flour

1 teaspoon vanilla

½ cup chopped pecans

"This Mincemeat Pie recipe of Nellie's has been a traditional Shoults family favorite for generations now... and it gets better every holiday season!"
Robbie Shoults

Preheat oven to 350 degrees. Put a sheet of aluminum foil over a baking pan. Set aside. In a saucepan, crumble the mincemeat. Add water and one cup sugar. Cook stirring constantly over medium heat for 5 minutes. Turn heat to low.

Add the flour to the remaining ¼ cup sugar. Stir well to blend. Slowly stir the sugar mixture into the mincemeat. Continue stirring and cook the mincemeat for about one minute or until thickened. Remove from heat. Add vanilla and nuts. Pour the mixture into the deep dish pie crust. Set aside.

Remove the other pie crust from its pan. Flatten the pie dough with a rolling pin. Place on top of the mincemeat. Cut around the edges leaving ½" of the pie dough beyond the bottom crust. Crimp the two edges together. Cut 4-6 slits in the top crust. Set the pie on top of the prepared baking pan. Bake 30-40 minutes or until top crust is golden. Let the pie cool before cutting. Serve with whipped cream if desired.

From the kitchen of Nellie Shoults

"Though the mountains be shaken and the hills be removed, yet my unfailing love for you will not be shaken nor my covenant of peace be removed,"
says the Lord, who has compassion on you.

Isaiah 54:10

I keep my eyes always on the Lord...
I will not be shaken.

Psalm 16:8

PEACH PIE

Makes 1 pie

½ cup butter or margarine, melted

1 cup flour

½ teaspoon baking powder

½ teaspoon salt

⅔ cup milk

2 cups sugar, divided

1 can peaches or cherries in natural juices, drain juice and reserve

Preheat oven to 350 degrees. Spray a 9" pie pan or baking dish with non-stick spray. Set aside. In mixing bowl, stir together one cup sugar, flour, salt, and baking powder. Stir in butter and milk. Mix to blend. Put mixture in the prepared pie pan and distribute to cover bottom of pan evenly. Put drained fruit on top of this mixture. Set aside. In a microwave safe bowl or measuring cup, mix reserved juices with remaining 1 cup sugar. Heat mixture in a microwave for 20-30 seconds. Stir until sugar is dissolved. Pour sweetened juices over pie surface. Bake pie for 45 minutes or until crust is golden brown.

- REMEMBERIN' BEAR BOTTOM BY HUNTER SHOULTS -

"Hard working and stubborn... That's what us Shoults men are known for!

I remember one year Dad was puttin' Christmas lights up on the house, like we used to!

Well he was bound and determined to finish before dark, and of course, here came 'A Turd Floater' (which is Texan for a really hard rain)!

Dad was mad cause he wanted to finish, and well it was gettin' dark too! So he thought it'd be smart to turn the lights on so he could see.

It wasn't 3 minutes into it that he drove a staple smack dab thru the middle of that Christmas light wire, shockin' him and knockin' him clean off that ladder!

Luckily, he wasn't hurt too bad... But, I still think to this day that's why we haven't had any Christmas lights up on the house ever since!"

NEIMAN'S $250 COOKIE RECIPE

Yields Approximately 112 Cookies

2 cups butter, softened

2 cups sugar

2 cups brown sugar

4 eggs

2 teaspoons vanilla

4 cups flour

5 cups rolled oats

1 teaspoon salt

2 teaspoons baking powder

2 teaspoons baking soda

24 ounces chocolate chips

1 *(8 ounce)* Hershey® bar, grated

3 cups chopped nuts

Preheat oven to 375 degrees.

Put rolled oats in a blender and blend until powdery. Place in a large bowl. Add flour, salt, baking powder, and baking soda. Stir to blend. Set aside.

In a large mixer bowl, cream butter with sugar and brown sugar. Add eggs, one at a time, mixing after each addition. Add vanilla. Add the flour mixture one cup at a time to the butter mixture. Beat to incorporate the flour after each addition. When all flour has been added, stir in the chips, grated chocolate bar, and nuts. Roll the dough into walnut sized balls and place 2" apart on an ungreased cookie sheet. Bake the cookies for 6-8 minutes or until lightly browned. Place a sheet of waxed paper on a flat kitchen work surface. Using a spatula, remove the cookies to the waxed paper. Allow the cookies to cool before storing in an airtight container.

- BEAR BOTTOM TALL TALES BY BOBBY SHOULTS -

"One year we had two floods in the same year! Water came up right across the highway!
It was so bad that our neighbors, the Chambers, had to move their furniture upstairs!
Water was so high that I had to get 'em in a boat and go through the upstairs window!
Chickens were stranded, so we had to put their feed on top of the barn to feed 'em!
That was a mess for a few weeks... but we all made it through it alright!"

NELLIE'S PIE CRUST

Makes 1 Crust

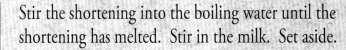

1¼ cups flour

7 Tablespoons solid shortening

3 Tablespoons water, boiling

1 Tablespoon milk

Nellie Shoults

Stir the shortening into the boiling water until the shortening has melted. Stir in the milk. Set aside.

Place the flour in a mixing bowl. Stir the shortening mixture into the flour. Mix well.

Place a sheet of waxed paper on a flat kitchen work surface. Turn the dough out onto the waxed paper. Place another sheet of waxed paper on top of the dough. With a rolling pin flatten the dough and roll to the desired thickness and shape for the pie crust. Remove the top layer of waxed paper. Gently lay the pie pan upside down on the dough. Work one of your hands under the bottom layer of waxed paper. Invert the dough and pan. Gently work the dough into the pan. Remove the layer of waxed paper. Cut the dough edges around the pan. Either fill the pie crust with your favorite fruit filling and bake; or fill with "pie beans" and bake prior to adding the filling of your choice.

From the kitchen of Nellie Shoults

DID YOU KNOW?

With personality and smiles to spare, Shoults family members have left their imprint on Texas, the region, and even the country! "If Hick and Nellie could only see the smokehouse now, and what their son Bobby, myself (their grandson), and Hunter (their great-grandson) were doing here, they'd be proud" Robbie said! "It seems like everything continues to blossom from the seeds that were planted over 70 years ago down on a farm in Bear Bottom, Texas!"

Strawberry Pie

Serves 8

9" baked pie crust

16 ounce carton of fresh strawberries, washed with tops removed

1 cup sugar

8 ounces cream cheese, softened

6 ounces Cool Whip®, defrosted

1 container strawberry glaze

Slice strawberries. Set aside.

In a small bowl blend sugar, cream cheese, and Cool Whip®. Spread the mixture evenly over the bottom of the baked pie crust. Top with sliced strawberries and distribute evenly over the cheese mixture. Spread the glaze over the strawberries, covering the entire surface of the pie. Chill well before cutting into serving pieces.

From the kitchen of Anita Overhultz

- Bear Bottom Ramblings By Robbie Shoults -

"When I was a kid, I looked forward to the balmy Bear Bottom summers with great anticipation! Not only was school out, but summertime also meant baby turkeys!!

I can remember spending the night with my grandparents and waking before sunrise to the sounds and smells of my grandmother, frying up some of our cured smokehouse bacon, rolling out some fresh biscuit dough and using that old metal buscuit cutter she so skillfully used, trying not to waste any... boy did MeMaw's cooking smell good!

However, this particular morning, breakfast was the last thing on my mind! I could hardly wait to walk up the hill with a flashlight to the turkey brooder houses! The further we walked the louder the chirping became, as my heart raced with excitement!

Finally, there they were, hatchery delivery vans that were loaded with boxes stacked high of day-old chirping hungry 'Poults' (baby turkeys)! And that was the beginning of my summers, cheerfully helping raise thousands of turkeys, later to become Holiday table centerpieces!"

PLAIN CAKE WITH FILLING

Serves 9

1 cup sugar

½ cup butter, softened

2 eggs

½ cup water

1⅔ cups flour

2 teaspoons baking powder

1 teaspoon vanilla

Filling

1 egg

⅓ cup sugar

Juice of one lemon

2 Tablespoons butter

1 Tablespoon flour

Preheat oven to 350 degrees. Spray a 9" x 9" baking dish with non-stick spray. Set aside.

Sift the flour and baking powder together. Set aside.

In a mixer bowl, combine sugar and butter. Beat on medium speed until well blended. Lower mixer speed and add eggs one at a time, beating after each addition. Add ½ of the flour mixture and mix until blended. Add ½ of the water, mixing to incorporate into the batter. Add remaining flour and mix well. Add remaining water and mix until blended. Add vanilla and mix to incorporate into the batter. Pour the batter into the prepared baking dish. Bake for 20-25 minutes or until cake tests done. Set aside to cool. Remove cake from pan.

While cake is baking, prepare the filling. Combine ingredients in a saucepan.

Cook over medium-low heat, stirring constantly, until mixture thickens. Remove from heat and beat with a whisk or fork.

Using a long-bladed bread knife, carefully cut the cake in half horizontally. Use the filling to cover one of the cut cake surfaces. Place the remaining half on top of the filling. Frost the cake with your favorite icing.

From the kitchen of Betty Parker

One thing I ask... that I may dwell in the house of the Lord all the days of my life, to gaze on the beauty of the Lord...

Psalm 27:4

PLAIN TEA CAKES

Makes approximately 3 dozen

1½ cups flour

¼ teaspoon salt

1½ teaspoon baking powder

1 egg

¼ cup butter, softened

½ cup sugar

3 Tablespoons milk

½ teaspoon vanilla or flavoring of your choice

"These Tea Cakes pair perfectly with a tall glass of milk or a cup of coffee, It's hard to find Tea Cakes these days so this recipe is perfect for that 'nostalgic craving'. All it takes is one bite to feel like you're a kid again!"
Stacia Shoults

Preheat oven to 350 degrees. Spray a cookie sheet with non-stick spray. Set aside.

Sift flour, salt, and baking powder together. Set aside.

In a mixing bowl, cream the butter and sugar together. Add the egg and beat until incorporated into the butter mixture. With the mixer on low speed, add ⅓ of the flour mixture beating until blended. Continue by adding ⅓ more of the flour mixture and beating well. Add remaining flour and beat until incorporated. Add the milk to the ingredients in the bowl and mix until blended. Place the dough on a clean, lightly floured kitchen work surface. Form the dough into a ball and flatten slightly with the palms of your hands. With a lightly floured rolling pin, roll the dough to ½" thick. Using a lightly floured biscuit cutter or round cookie cutter, cut the dough into circles. Place the dough circles on the prepared cookie sheet and bake for 8-10 minutes or until lightly browned. Cool on a wire rack to room temperature. If desired, dust with confectioner's sugar or frost with your favorite icing.

From the kitchen of Reece Brooks II

Consider the blameless, observe the upright; a future awaits those who seek peace.

Psalm 37:37

SAND TARTS

Makes approximately 2 dozen cookies

2 cups flour

½ cup solid shortening

1 cup sugar

1½ teaspoons baking powder

1 egg

¼ teaspoon ground cinnamon

"These Sand Tarts are so addicting! I use heart shaped cookie cutters to make them. Cooper and I will eat these at our very 'fancy' living room floor Tea Parties!"

Stacia Shoults

Preheat oven to 350 degrees. Spray a cookie sheet with non-stick spray. Set aside.

In a mixer bowl, blend sugar with the egg. Beat in the shortening until well blended. Set aside.

Sift the flour, baking powder, and cinnamon together. With the mixer on low speed, add the dry ingredients slowly to the shortening mixture, beating until all dry ingredients are blended into the dough. Put the cookie dough onto a clean kitchen work surface that has been lightly floured. Work the dough into a ball, then flatten the dough using your hands. With a rolling pin, roll the dough to a thickness of ¼". Cut with a lightly floured cookie or biscuit cutter. Place the cut-out cookie dough on the prepared cookie sheet. Bake the cookies for 10-15 minutes or until the cookies are lightly browned. Place a sheet of waxed paper on a clean kitchen work surface. Using a spatula transfer the cookies to the sheet waxed paper to cool. If desired, the cookies can be dusted with confectioner's sugar.

From the kitchen of Wilma Dorsey Stracner

For I am convinced that neither death nor life, neither angels nor demons, neither the present nor the future, nor any powers, neither height nor depth, nor anything else in all creation, will be able to separate us from the love of God that is in Christ Jesus our Lord.

Romans 8:38-39

"Hunter and I feel so blessed
to be a part of the Shoults
family legacy!"
Stacia Shoults

Hunter & Stacia Shoults

TUNNEL OF FUDGE CAKE

Serves 12

1½ cups butter, at room temperature

1½ cups sugar

6 eggs, at room temperature

2 cups flour, sifted

1 package fudge frosting mix

2 cups chopped walnuts

"This Tunnel Of Fudge Cake recipe of Anita's is a Chocolate lover's dream come true! Every time I serve it to family and friends, I always get requests for second helpings!"
Brenda Shoults

Preheat oven to 350 degrees. Grease and flour a Bundt® or tube cake pan. Set aside.

In a large mixer bowl, cream the butter and sugar together. Add the eggs one at a time, beating after each addition. Beat at high speed for 1-2 minutes until the mixture is light and fluffy. Lower the mixer speed and add the frosting mix. While the mixer is on low speed, gradually add the flour. When all flour is incorporated into the batter, turn off the mixer. By hand, fold in the chopped nuts. Pour the batter into the prepared pan. Bake for an hour or until the cake tests done. Cool on a wire rack for two hours. Remove the cake from the pan and allow it to cool to room temperature before serving.

From the kitchen of Anita Overhultz

DID YOU KNOW?

The Caddo Indians once inhabited much of what is now the Piney Woods region of East Texas!

By around 800 AD, this society had begun to coalesce into the Caddoan culture. Some villages began to gain prominence as ritual centers, where major earthworks were built, serving as temple mounds and elite residences. These mounds were arranged around leveled, large open plazas used for ceremonies.

By around 1200 AD, the Caddo world had developed many artisans and craftsmen in their villages, many who had developed their artistic skills and earthwork mound-building talents into a flourishing crescendo during the 12th and 13th centuries!

Pottery shards, arrow heads and other relics from this era have even been found in Bear Bottom!

CHUNKY PEANUT BRITTLE

Makes 2½ pounds

1½ cups butter, plus 1½ teaspoons butter to grease the pan

2 cups peanut butter chips, divided

1¾ cups sugar

3 Tablespoons light corn syrup

3 Tablespoons water

1½ cups salted peanuts, coarsely chopped

½ cup semi-sweet chocolate chips

"This is a family favorite around Bear Bottom!"
Stacia Shoults

Butter the bottom and sides of a 15" x 10" x 1" pan with the 1½ teaspoons butter. Sprinkle one cup of peanut butter chips evenly over the bottom of the pan. Set aside. In a heavy saucepan, bring sugar, corn syrup, water, and 1½ cups butter to boil over medium heat, stirring constantly. When the butter has melted, stop stirring and insert a candy thermometer. Cook without stirring until the temperature of 300 degrees is reached. Remove pan from heat and stir in peanuts. Quickly pour mixture into the prepared pan. Spread the brittle to cover the bottom of the pan. Sprinkle with chocolate chips and remaining peanut butter chips. When the chips start melting take a butter knife and gently swirl the softened chips over the top of the brittle. Set aside to cool before breaking into pieces. Store brittle in an airtight container.

From the kitchen of Laurie Stacy

- REMEMBERIN' BEAR BOTTOM BY HUNTER SHOULTS -

"I remember the time we went to Nebraska to go talk to Cabela's about their order. We were lookin' 'round knowin' we had a huntin' trip to Alaska comin' up. I found a Winchester 300 short mag camo that I wanted real bad! I asked Poppa if he'd get it for me and he said... 'Ah no boy you don't need that thing' so I sulked around for awhile, then asked him again, tellin' him I'd get a job to pay him back. My hair was shoulder length back then, so he said 'If you'll get that nappy hair cut off your head, I'll get it for you!' That summer, with my freshly cut hair, I carried my new Winchester 300 to Alaska, where we all hunted together!"

BeeBee's Famous Banana Pudding

Makes 12-14 servings

1 large box instant vanilla pudding mix

3 cups Pet® milk

1 can sweetened condensed milk

12 ounce tub Cool Whip®, thawed

½ cup Coffee Mate®

Several bananas, sliced

1 box vanilla wafers

"This is the 'essential' Banana Pudding recipe of BeeBee's. Her Banana Pudding has always been my favorite, ever since I can remember!"
Hunter Shoults

In a large mixer bowl, beat the pudding mix with Pet® milk until the mixture thickens. Add the condensed milk, Cool Whip®, and Coffee Mate®. Mix well. Set aside. In a large serving dish, place a layer of vanilla wafers. Top the wafers with banana slices. Spoon the pudding mixture over the top. If you have more wafers, place them over the top of the pudding. Cover with plastic wrap and refrigerate. Chill the dish for at least 2 hours before serving.

From the kitchen of Brenda Shoults

Pound Cake

Makes 1 cake

16 ounce bag of confectioner's sugar

1 pound of flour, sifted

6 eggs at room temperature

3 sticks butter, softened

1 teaspoon lemon juice

1 Tablespoon vanilla

"A delicious Pound Cake all by itself or to use for strawberry shortcake!"
Tracy Shoults

Preheat oven to 325 degrees. Grease and flour the loaf pan you choose to use. Set aside. In a large mixer bowl, cream the butter and sugar until fluffy. Add eggs, one at a time beating after each addition. Gradually add flour while mixing on low speed. Add lemon juice and vanilla. Beat on medium speed for one minute. Pour cake batter into the prepared pan. Bake for one hour to 1½ hours *(depending on the size pan you use)* or until the cake tests done. Set pan on wire racks to cool for 10 minutes. Remove cake from the pan and continue cooling to room temperature.

"*Nothing is quite as tranquil or beautiful,
as a Texas sunrise over Bear Bottom!*"
Robbie Shoults

Momma Dorsey's Cake & Icing

Serves 10

2 Tablespoons solid shortening or butter, softened

1 teaspoon baking powder

¾ cup sugar

1 cup flour

1 egg

½ cup milk

½ teaspoon vanilla

⅛ teaspoon salt

Icing:

1 teaspoon light corn syrup

1 Tablespoon butter, melted

½ teaspoon vanilla

1 cup sugar

½ cup milk

Preheat oven to 325 degrees. Spray an 8" x 8" glass baking dish with non-stick spray. Set aside.

In a mixer bowl, combine all ingredients. With mixer on low, beat about one minute to thoroughly moisten dry ingredients. Increase mixer speed to medium-high and beat the cake batter for two minutes.

Pour into prepared dish and bake for 20-25 minutes or until cake tests done.

Prepare icing. Blend all ingredients in a mixer bowl and beat until smooth.

Frost cake with icing when the cake has cooled slightly.

"This simple cake and icing of Momma Dorsey's has always been special to me!"

Robbie Shoults

DID YOU KNOW?

Bear Creek Smokehouse was named 'Family Business of the Year' by the U.S. Small Business Administration in the spring of 2013.

A representative from the Administration came from Washington D.C. to Arlington, Texas for the awards ceremony to meet the Shoults family and to invite them to Washington D.C., to meet with and serve smokehouse selections to state directors and congressmen at America's Small Business Development Center. Robbie said, "In 2015, we took our food up to Washington and showed them how we do it in Bear Bottom!" While there, Robbie spoke to the Senators about the association with the Small Business Administration. Their visit was such a hit, that the family was invited back for an encore in 2016!

DEVIL'S FOOD CAKE

Serves 10-12

1 cup butter, softened

2½ cups sugar

5 eggs at room temperature

3 cups flour

¼ cup cocoa powder

1 teaspoon baking powder

2 teaspoons baking soda

¼ teaspoon salt

1 cup buttermilk

Minute Fudge Icing:

½ cup cocoa

¾ cup butter

¾ cup milk

3 cups sugar

⅛ teaspoon salt

1 cup chopped nuts, optional

"Chocolate is my number one weakness, followed in short order by just about anything sweet on the planet! This Devil's Food Cake recipe does not disappoint!"
Stacia Shoults

Preheat oven to 350 degrees. Spray four (9") cake pans with non-stick spray. Set aside.

Sift the flour, cocoa powder, baking powder, baking soda, and salt together. Set aside.

In a large mixer bowl, beat the butter and sugar together until light and fluffy. Add the eggs one at a time beating after each addition. Alternately add ⅓ of the flour mixture and ⅓ of the buttermilk, beating with the mixer on low speed after each addition. When the flour and buttermilk are incorporated into the batter, beat for an additional two minutes with the mixer on medium speed. Divide the batter evenly among the prepared pans. Bake for 18-20 minutes or until the cakes test done. Let cool on wire racks for 10 minutes. Remove the cakes from the pans and allow them to cool to room temperature. At this point, the cakes can be wrapped tightly in plastic wrap and refrigerated or frozen until you are ready to assemble the cake.

In a medium saucepan, combine cocoa, sugar, and salt. Stir in milk and heat over medium heat stirring constantly. Cook until thickened. Stir in butter. Beat the icing with a whisk until creamy. If you are using nuts, stir them into the frosting at this time or sprinkle them over cake immediately after frosting has been applied.

FALLEN CAKE

Serves 6-8

1 box Duncan Hines® butter cake mix

3 eggs, divided

1 stick butter, melted

1 box confectioner's sugar

8 ounces cream cheese, softened

1 cup chopped pecans, divided

1 teaspoon almond extract

"This irresistible Fallen Cake recipe, with its tongue-in-cheek name, is one of the most scrumptious cake's I've ever tasted!"
Brenda Shoults

Preheat oven to 350 degrees. Spray a 13" x 9" oven-safe dish with non-stick spray. Set aside.

In a mixer bowl, blend cake mix with one egg and melted butter. Mix on medium speed for two minutes. Pour the batter into the prepared pan and spread evenly. Set aside.

In a mixer bowl, blend confectioner's sugar, two eggs, cream cheese, ½ cup of the chopped pecans, and almond extract. Mix to blend until smooth. Pour over the cake batter. Sprinkle the remaining chopped pecans evenly over the top. Bake for 10 minutes and lower oven temperature to 325 degrees. Cook for an additional 30-35 minutes or until cake tests done. Allow to cool before serving.

From the kitchen of Mary L. Carrington

DID YOU KNOW?

Agriculture has been the core of the Shoults family's existence for over 100 years and counting! Robbie's great grandfather began buying land in Harrison County in 1902! His grandfather, Hick, was also active in a (newly formed) Agriculture Youth Organization, the 4H Club!

It was also a great, great Uncle, who at the time was an Agriculture teacher, that advised Hick, in 1943 to start raising turkeys, in addition to his other farming activities. Robbie's dad, Bobby, was also involved in 4H and Future Farmers Of America from an early age!

Robbie and his son, Hunter, continue to utilize the skills learned from the leadership development, cooperative activities, and practical Agriculture training that were important initiatives for so many rural youth involved in those organizations!

Bobby Shoults
Vice-Pres
55-56
VOCATIONAL
FFA
AGRICULTURE
VOCATIONAL
FFA
AGRICULTURE
Robbie Shoults
President
Hunter Shoults
AGRICULTURAL
FFA
EDUCATION

Hunter, Robbie, Bobby & Barrett Shoults

BROWNIES

Makes 12-16 brownies

1 cup butter or margarine

4 squares unsweetened chocolate

4 eggs

¼ teaspoon salt

2 cups sugar

1 cup sifted flour

2 teaspoons vanilla

2 cups chopped pecans

"Hunter and I made a batch of these Brownies on our honymoon in Colorado. This recipe reminds me of sitting by the fireplace with hot brownies, smothered in homemade vanilla ice cream, watching the snow fall!"

Stacia Shoults

Preheat oven to 350 degrees. Spray a 9" x 9" baking dish with non-stick spray. Set aside.

In a saucepan, melt butter with chocolate squares. Set aside.

In a mixing bowl, beat the eggs until frothy. Add sugar and salt. Mix to blend well. Add the melted butter mixture. Mix to blend. Add the flour and mix until smooth. Stir in the vanilla and pecans. Pour the batter into the prepared baking dish and bake for 20-25 minutes or until the brownies test done. Set aside to cool to room temperature before cutting into serving pieces. Store the brownies in an airtight container.

"When the Coreopsis blooms appear,
our mid-summer pastures are set ablaze
with a beautiful golden hue!"

Robbie Shoults

- ACKNOWLEDGEMENTS & THANKS -

We Would Like To Give Special Thanks The People And Companies Who Have Contributed To Making This Cookbook Dream A Reality!

- CHUCK STOVALL - DYOFILOS, LLC -
Content Editing, Design, Photo And Art Direction

- JIM BOWIE - JIM BOWIE PHOTOGRAPHY, INC. -
Food Studio Photography

- JARED NAVARRE -
Location Photography

- LINDA BELLINGHAM -
Recipe Conversions, Editing And Food Styling

- ADOBE STOCK® & DREAMSTIME® -
Various Other Food, Location Photography And Graphic Elements

- WIKIPEDIA® -
Various Texas Historical Information And Fine Art

- ADDITIONAL CONTRIBUTORS -
Bobby Shoults, Brenda Shoults, Robbie Shoults, Tracy Shoults, Stacia Shoults, Hunter Shoults And Mike Whyte, Bear Creek Smokehouse - Various Recipes, Tall Tales, Ramblings And Rememberin's, As Well As Other Historical Shoults Family And Bear Creek Smokehouse Information Including The Shreveport Times.
Various Other Recipe Contributors - Previously Acknowledged With Their Respective Recipe Contributions
Kimberli Burns - Special Digital File Production Assistant
Theo Regas, Dyofilos, LLC - Food Photography Coordination And Administration
Melissa Yount - Assistant Food Stylist, Cyndi McDonnell - Prop Styling/Coordinator And Assistant Food Stylist
The Shreveport Times And Dana Goolsby - www.myetex.com

- A WORD ABOUT ACCURACY -
We Have Made Every Attempt To Be As Accurate As Possible On All Recipes And Information In This Cookbook. Any Error Is Purely Unintentional. If You Find Any Error, Please Let Us Know, And We Will Gladly Correct The Error For Future Printings Of This Cookbook. These Are Family Recipes Handed Down From One Generation To The Next. Every Oven Is Unique, Therefore; Adjustments To Cooking Times May Be Necessary For Each Individual Oven. Bear Creek Smokehouse Or Any Of Its Successors Or Assigns Are Not Responsible For Any Inaccuracies.

WEIGHTS, MEASURES & CONVERSIONS

1/16 teaspoon	A dash
1/8 teaspoon	A pinch
3 teaspoons	1 Tablespoon
1/8 cup	2 tablespoons (= *1 standard coffee scoop*)
1/4 cup	4 Tablespoons
1/3 cup	5 Tablespoons plus 1 teaspoon
1/2 cup	8 Tablespoons
3/4 cup	12 Tablespoons
1 cup	16 Tablespoons
1 pound	16 ounces
8 Fluid ounces	1 cup
1 Pint	2 Cups (= *16 fluid ounces*)
1 Quart	2 Pints (= *4 cups*)
1 Gallon	4 Quarts (= *16 cups*)

1 T	1 Tablespoon
1 stick	8 Tablespoons (= *1/2 cup*)
4 sticks	32 Tablespoons
Half and half	1/2 milk 1/2 cream
Heavy cream	Whipping cream
275º F	140º C
300º F	150º C
325º F	165º C
350º F	180º C
375º F	190º C
400º F	200º C
425º F	220º C
450º F	230º C
475º F	240º C

NOTES

INDEX

DESSERTS *(Continued)*

Pecan Pie 173
Plain Cake With Filling 186
Plain Tea Cakes 187
Pound Cake 193
Praline Thumbprint Cookies 155
Pumpkin Swirl Cheesecake 153
Sand Tarts 188
Snicker® Cinna'mores 177
Sopapilla Cheesecake 157
Strawberry Pie 184
Tunnel Of Fudge Cake 191

MEATS

Baked Mushroom Meat Loaf 113
Beef Tips 95
Chicken Cordon Bleu 92
Chicken Enchilurritos 114
Chicken Excelsior House 104
Chicken-Fried Steak & Gravy 98
Chicken Tetrazzini 115
Gemini Moon Pebbles *(Bean Burgers)* 105
Marilyn's No-Fry Baked Chicken Breasts 99
Our Favorite Meat Loaf 110
Parmesan Chicken 101
Pork Carnitas 116
Pork Chop Supreme 107
Salisbury Steak 94
Stacia's Chicken Supreme 100
Stuffed Peppers 106
Sweet & Spicy Bacon Chicken 111

SALADS

Avocado Tomato Salad 28
Broccoli Salad 25
Chicken Salad 29
Corn, Spinach & Cherry Tomato Salad 30
Fresh Apple Salad 27
Frozen Fruit Salad 22
Hot Chicken Salad 27
Layered Salad 28
Mixed Vegetable Salad 24
Orange Jell-O® Salad 29
Oriental Chicken Salad 36
Strawberry Jell-O® Salad 25

SNACKS

Avocado Salsa 17
Bear Bottom Bites 5
Cranberry-Glazed Appetizer Meatballs 2
Creamed Pimento Cheese 3
Cucumbers In Vinegar 10
Curry Dip 14
Fresh Tomato Relish 6
Frosted Peanuts 20
Guacamole 14
Marinated Carrots 17
Mini Pizzas 12
Mississippi Sin 3
Pâté Of Chicken Livers 6
Pink Dip 9
Sadie's Texas Pizza 13
Spinach Balls 7
Stacia's Skinny Dipping 5
Tangy Cheese Ball 10

SOUPS

Broccoli Cheese Soup 39
Cheesy Chicken Soup 43
Kennie's Taco Soup 42
Potato Soup 42, 44
Spicy Chicken Soup 38
Vegetable Beef Soup 44

VEGGIES

Au Gratin Potatoes With Smoked Ham 130
Bacon Wrapped Green Beans 142
Baked Squash 131
Brenda's Squash Casserole 135
Broccoli Rigatoni 141
Cheesy Mashed Potatoes 118
Corn Casserole 127
Creamy Squash 131
Decorated Corn 120
English Peas & Peppered Bacon 118
Green Rice Dressing 119
Jalapeño Rice 120
Laredo Ranch Beans 136
Merry Squash Bake 129
Mexican Street Corn 140
Potato Casserole 126, 137

VEGGIES *(Continued)*

Scalloped Potatoes 121
Scalloped Potatoes & Ham 132
Spicy Purple Hull Peas 126
Spicy Sautéed Green Beans 119
Squash Dressing 129
Stir-Fried Cabbage 124
String Bean & English Pea Casserole 121
Super Garlic & Rosemary New Potatoes 134
Zippy Zucchini Skillet 139

NOTES

NOTES

NOTES

NOTES

NOTES

NOTES

NOTES

"*Plant the seed, work it, daily nurturing and caring for it, with all the love and care you can give, and eventually it will be a perfect reflection of you and of all of your diligent endeavors!*"

Unknown